Embraced by Grace

Small Group Study Guide

Written by Salina Duffy

Contributors: Amy Ford & Jacqueline Fox

iembracegrace.com
gatewaycreate.com
gatewaypeople.com

Table of Contents

Embrace Grace Heartbeat

When *Embrace Grace* began in 2008, our very first semester we had 3 sweet mommas with babies growing in their bellies. Each girl was so unique and beautiful. Getting to know them was like opening a treasure box and finding out about their lives, what they had been through and how much stronger they were becoming because of it. Each of them had a story that was their very own with different situations, but one thing they all had in common was HOPE.

With every semester since, as *Embrace Grace* has grown and we've had many girls come through our classes, semester after semester and year after year, one common thing has bound us all together … it's hope. Yes, things might just be crumbling around you and you feel like you can't see how everything is going to work out for your future, but it will. We've seen countless girls with those exact feelings, but then we got to watch all the amazing miracles God did over the course of the pregnancy and even beyond.

We strongly believe that you are not holding this book by accident. God connected people, aligned everything just right so that you would be invited to join this adventure with Him. He wants to blow you away with His love so that you will never ever be the same again. He wants to lift you up so that you don't have to go through this pregnancy feeling broken, sad, angry, confused or scared. He wants to take care of you and for you to just trust Him!

As you read through this book over the next few months, you will notice a common theme of "TION" words.

God has given us the unction to set some things in motion. We have a notion to turn things around. We want to have a "no-shun" set in action. This pun is intended: No Shun Allowed!

Shun synonyms: to avoid, ignore, turn back on, refuse, reject, rejection, scorn

This is a different kind of "TION"—it's a "SHUN." Have you ever been shunned? Have you ever had a feeling people are saying, "Look over there, look at her …" Maybe pointing fingers? Maybe placing blame and making you feel ashamed or guilty? Maybe you feel rejected or ignored. We have a notion to turn that around. We want to embrace you with grace.

Notion [noh-sh*uh*n] definition: an idea, opinion, whim
Notion synonyms: conception, intuition, indication

For far too long, people, and sadly sometimes even the church, have shunned the single pregnant ladies. We have sent them off to look for support somewhere else. We, the church, should be the ones reaching out to them, encouraging them, embracing them and loving them as they have made the brave and courageous choice to carry this precious life inside of them.

Our desire is to see others no longer shun the single and pregnant, but instead to allow them to be embraced by grace. To shower them with grace! Grace extended from leaders, grace extended from the church, grace extended from pastors and teachers, grace extended from parents and family members, grace extended from our nation, and grace extended from the world. We can change the world two heartbeats at a time—the mommies' and the babies' heartbeats.

We have exchanged the shun for lots of …*tions* that will empower, encourage, enlighten, envelop, engage and embrace in a whole new way. Each chapter will be titled with a…*tion* word. These …*tions* will bring forth sentiments and keepsakes that will be treasured in your heart and others' for a lifetime.

Only *...tions* here—Habitation, Realization, Perception, Expectation, Revelation, Conviction, Vindication and Transformation. And then we end the semester with God's greatest gift, GRACE. You are welcomed here with arms open wide. You are covered in God's loving embrace and His GRACE!

We pray that God writes upon the hearts of each and every one of you that opens up the pages of this book. We pray that you would be touched and that you would open up your heart for God to heal all the broken places and for you to accept His free gift of grace. This will be a time of reflection, recollection and illumination that will brighten your days and your new life after the baby. We love you so much and pray for all of you often. We are excited you have chosen to embark upon this journey, and we have such awesome expectation of how your life will never be the same as you begin to put your trust in God.

We can't wait to hear the stories of transformation!

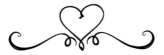

Amy's Heartbeat

I remember the feeling like it was yesterday … alone, scared, worried, hopeless. I was only 19. Pregnant. So many thoughts and fears swarmed my head constantly, trying to push me to the edge of no return. I thought that maybe an abortion was the answer to all of my problems. Even though I knew in my heart it was wrong, maybe I could just deal with the consequences of a broken heart later.

After. It could be a quick fix. I wouldn't have to tell my parents. I wouldn't be kicked out and homeless. My boyfriend thought for sure that he would have to drop out of college because his dad would surely cut him off financially. Our lives would be ruined.

I was robotic in my movement and intention, trying to brush away any connection I felt with this child growing inside me. I wouldn't let my emotions show; it hurt too much. My boyfriend made the appointment for me at the abortion clinic. My head wanted to get rid of my problem any way I could, but my heart wasn't cooperating as much.

Sitting in that cold, sterile clinic, I heard the nurse explain to me how I was over 6 weeks pregnant and the different abortion methods. I tried to push down the lump in my throat. I tried to think about how this was for the best. I tried to blink back the tears. I tried to take deep breaths to calm my rising heart rate, but the more I tried, the faster everything caved in on me at once. All the emotion I had been pushing back for the past week came rushing over me. The room began to spin, and then everything went black. Silence.

Seconds later, as if someone was slowly turning up the volume on a radio, I could hear voices. Women I didn't recognize were saying my name. I blinked my eyes a few times and looked around to try to process what had happened. A nurse was leaning over me, fanning me. Another nurse was holding a cup of water, trying to get me to hydrate. *What had happened?* They said I had fainted.

The memories started flooding back in. Pregnant. Abortion. Vacuum method. Tears started rolling down my cheeks, and my heart sank again as I realized I was pregnant— talking to a nurse about abortion. I tried so hard to hold back my sobs. *There is a baby inside of me. How will I ever be able to go through with this?* The nurse interrupted my thoughts, "You are too emotionally distraught to have an abortion today. You can come back and reschedule another time, but you are just too upset to make a decision like this today."

God promises to turn ALL things for good for those that love Him

Overwhelming fear came over me as I walked out that day, but an odd feeling of relief set in at the same time. I decided in that moment that I had to find a way to figure this out. I had no idea how I would provide for a baby. I had no idea where I would live. I had no idea how I would find childcare or a job. I just hoped and prayed that it would all work itself out. I needed God more than ever. I knew I couldn't live my life the way I had been, trying to figure everything out on my own. Lost.

Seven and a half months later, I had a son. He was beautiful. Blonde hair and blue eyes. Tiny cleft in his chin. Beautiful hands that wrapped around my finger perfectly. Tiny toes that curled when I rubbed the bottom of his foot. I had never loved anything so much in my life. He was mine. Out of all the girls in the whole world, God chose me. ME! He chose me to be this baby boy's mother. God has a plan for this baby's life. He has a plan for MY life. He has a plan for your life, too!

My son ended up being the best thing that ever happened to me. Looking back, I have no idea where I would be if I had gone back for that abortion. My life would look a lot different than it does now. Before, I searched everywhere I knew to just feel whole and happy. I mean, everywhere! But what I was lacking all along was that close relationship with my heavenly Father. And then, right when my life seemed the most chaotic and I was spending all my time searching for something that was right in front of me the whole time, God gave me a precious, miracle baby. God turned what I thought was one of the most difficult seasons of my life, into a beautiful story full of purpose and grace.

Even though you are experiencing an unplanned pregnancy, I want you to know that God DID plan this life inside of you. He has a destiny and a purpose for your child, and it is an awesome one! If things seem out of order and you can't see beyond these nine months of pregnancy and what it will look like after that, God does. Every question that you might have about finances, a home, a job, childcare, the baby's daddy, your future husband … God already has the answer. Just trust Him and lean on Him during this season. Just take a deep breath and take this one day at a time. The good news is that you don't have to have your life plan mapped out right now.

There is so much for you beyond what is going on right now. I know it's hard to see past this, but God promises to turn ALL things for good for those that love Him. He will turn this very situation you are going through right now, for good. He is FOR you!

I remember my pregnancy being a little lonely at times. I know it wasn't because my friends didn't like me anymore. Looking back, I can see it was more about them not knowing what to say. It was like the "elephant in the room." Do they call you and say, "Congratulations!" or "I'm sorry …" They don't really know, so a lot of times they quit calling. (Usually they come back after you have the baby, and hopefully by then, you can determine if they are the kind of friend you even would like to have.)

We hope this semester you connect with NEW friends—girls who are in the same spot as you, with maybe a very different story than yours, but one big thing in common with you, HOPE. We hope you feel comfortable enough with your leaders to ask questions, study God's Word and let God's love reach out to you even through them as well. Open up to them and share your heart. You will be surprised to know that they may have been through the very same thing you have; just ask!

Most importantly, we hope and pray that during this semester, those of you who do not know God as your personal Lord and Savior, will invite Him into your hearts and begin a new life full of hope and promise for your future AND your baby growing inside you. And for those of you who may have accepted Him before but feel disconnected from your heavenly Father because of all the distractions of the world, we pray that God radically draws close to you as you draw close to Him. We pray that you can block out all the "noise" of the world and learn how to tune in to His voice. He loves you so much. He has been waiting for this moment, the moment you begin to spend time with Him and get to know Him by His Word (the Bible) and His voice.

If you open your heart and have an open mind, this could be the best time of your life, a season of miracles and blessings! Let God's love wash over you and heal every area of your heart. Whether you are pregnant and choosing adoption or keeping your baby, God is right there with you. He is whispering His secrets to you, guiding and leading you to the amazing destiny He has for you.

Salina's Heartbeat

I am a baby lover! I always longed to be a mommy for as long as I can remember. At such an early age, my desire was to have a baby. When asked by my teachers, *"What do you want to be when you grow up?"* my response was always, *"To be a mommy and have babies."* I babysat as much as I could when I was younger just to be around the little ones. I was even a nanny for a baby boy for over a year. I ABSOLUTELY LOVE BABIES!

I just can't get enough! I love everything about babies from the tops of their heads to their wiggly toes. Kisses always flow when babies are around. I just can't help myself! If I could just sit and hold a baby all day long, that would satisfy my heart's desire.

I met the love of my life on my 18th birthday and graduation day. It was love at first sight. I was sitting in front of the fireplace at my best friend's house, and as the front door opened and our eyes met, I knew he was the one I was going to marry. He walked over to me by the fire and said the sweetest things to me. I smiled. He smiled. We were smitten. We went out on our very first date the next day and have been together ever since! As I am writing this, we are celebrating our 17th wedding anniversary in 2 weeks. Our love has grown deeper and stronger each and every day!

Being married and settled into our home, all of those mommy desires I've always had really started bubbling up inside of me. I was longing for the day I'd get to hold my baby, and that day could not come soon enough for me. My hubby had a few timelines in place that he wanted to follow before we started a family. It was logical, and I understood, for a while, but my heart kept longing for a baby. We began to attend marriage counseling together to express our hearts' desires and longings and how we could both relate with each other's feelings. He was to write out his thoughts and reasonings, and I was to write out mine. This was a type of heart release for the both of us. I shed lots of tears. My questions were "Why? Why not now? How long must I wait? We have been married two years."

About a year later, I was feeling a little different than normal. My sister was at my home with me, and I took a pregnancy test. It was positive! I was pregnant! I was elated and full of joy! My dreams were finally coming true! Thoughts like, "*I have a baby growing inside of me. This is really happening! I am going to be a Mommy! I can't wait!*" My heart was so happy! I went to the store and bought a stuffed angel and the largest "Daddy" pin that I could find. I went home, and my thoughts turned from excitement to a little bit of nervousness. I was wondering how he was going to take the news.

When he came home, I gave him his gifts with a big hopeful smile on my face. He looked at me and patted my tummy and said, "So, we have a baby in there ... Congratulations!" It took him a few hours to adjust to the shock, and then he was so excited! Probably even more so than I was. He completely took all of his timelines, reasonings and things he had written down of what he wanted to accomplish before becoming a daddy, and threw them out the window. He felt ready to be a Daddy!

Nine months later, we held our precious baby boy, Landan Taylor, in our arms. Tears of joy streamed down our faces as we looked into the eyes of our sweet baby. He was ours. Forever. A sweet miracle.

Even though I was married, I can somewhat relate with the feelings that you may have experienced when you first found out you were pregnant. I had thoughts like, *What is my baby's daddy going to say? How is he going to react? Will he take the news well? Is he ready to be a daddy? Well, ready or not, here baby comes!* Please know that you are not alone!

Soon after Landan was born, my husband was the one that actually suggested trying for another baby. I was so surprised, but excited! We were joyful and expectant. We had gotten pregnant so easy with our first. Why should it be any different with our second? A month went by, then two months, then six, and still no baby. We were hounded by doubts—*What are we doing wrong? We know what it takes to make a baby. We are following the steps. Why is it not happening this time? We are ready, so ready.* With each passing month, my hubby would walk up to me expectant, but I would just shake my head no, not this month. We both had tears. A year went by, then two years. *How long, Lord? How long must we be patient and wait?*

We never gave up hope. We just kept praying and believing … but with each month passing by, that longing for a baby was becoming more and more unfulfilled. Every wish that our firstborn son could make, he would wish for a baby brother. Blowing out candles on his birthday cake, "I wish for a baby brother!" Throwing pennies in the fountains, "I wish for a baby brother." He made wishes upon shooting stars. He kept praying, hoping and wishing for a baby brother over and over again. It was all he could think about. After four years of infertility, our hopes were still to conceive and have a baby.

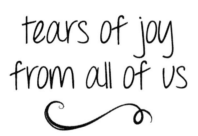

On Mother's Day 2006, I told my husband that I wanted our family to try a new church, Gateway Church. We walked in the doors, and a flood of emotions came over me. I felt at home the moment we walked in. So did Cory. We held hands and felt such peace. Worship was so moving and touching. Everything felt so right, so perfect, like this was what we had been searching for all along and finally we had found it. Pastor Robert spoke a powerful message about the enemy of devotion. He shared how the enemy can come in and even rob mothers of their joy on Mother's Day. There was a video montage of mothers and their little ones on the screen, and a sense of mixed emotions arose inside of me. My heart was happy, but would also cringe at the same time. *Why was my womb still empty? Why had I not been able to conceive again?* These were the questions arising in my mind as I watched the video. At the end of the service, Pastor Robert asked if there were any women that had been trying to get pregnant and unable to conceive to stand if they would like to receive prayer. Immediately I stood, without hesitation or a second thought. He prayed a powerful prayer over the women who were standing with me. We were all in the same place, longing for a child.

After the service, I went to the altar for prayer. I walked to a sweet pastor and his wife who were up front. She held out her hands, and I placed my hands in hers. Tears began to fall as I shared my heart's cry with her. She prayed the most amazing heartfelt prayer over me that I will cherish forever. She spoke a phrase that my heart held onto and I can still hear ringing in my ears. *"God, you give us the desires of our hearts; and by* **next Mother's Day**, *may Salina not only have one little boy to run after, but a new baby in her arms to hold."* As tears streamed down my face, I embraced her and thanked her for the encouraging and hopeful prayer. I felt at that moment a miracle was going to happen. I could not see it. I did not know when it was going to happen, but I believed. That's what faith is all about. Believing even when you do not see.

Three months later, the pregnancy stick finally read positive! We were having a baby! This time I surprised my hubby by wrapping the pregnancy test in tissue paper and handing the test to him as I sat at the bottom of the staircase. He embraced me, and tears streamed down both our faces. Our prayers had been answered. All in God's timing!

I loved everything about my pregnancy! I wanted to somehow freeze time and keep him in my tummy where I knew he was so safe and tucked in so warmly, but at the same time could not wait for him to finally be delivered so I could hold him. True to the prayer that was prayed over us, our baby boy was born 4 days before Mother's Day 2007. He was 2 days past due and had to be induced, but he was so worth the wait! Our hopes, dreams, prayers and wishes all came true the moment he was born. Our hearts were so full of joy. Cory and Landan were the best coaches in the hospital room with me. They told me when to push and when to relax. They were such great encouragers! I will forever cherish the looks on their faces when Logan was born—tears of joy from all of us, love at first sight for this precious miracle baby boy.

Ecclesiastes 3 declares that there is a time for everything. A time to be born. A time to embrace. God has been revealing and unfolding His plans and purpose for my life little by little. With everything I've been through, He was preparing me for such a time as this. This is my time to embrace the mommies and babies in the womb. To embrace the babies everywhere. To pray daily for mommies to choose life. For mommies' and daddies' hearts to soften. For abortions to stop. For babies' voices to be heard. My alarm is set for 11:11 every day, reminding me to pray for the babies to be saved. I pray for a force field to be placed around the wombs. I believe and know that God is hearing our prayers. I believe that we can change the world 2 heartbeats at a time—the mommies' and the babies' heartbeats together. God's heartbeat combined with our heartbeats and theirs.

I long for my heart to beat so closely with God's. My very first experience of this was during a Pink Impact Conference back in 2008. Kari Jobe was leading worship, and God's presence was so intense, and we were fully engaged in the heart of God. Kari was singing, "I want to sit at your feet, drink from the cup in your hand, lay back against you and breathe, and feel your heartbeat …" At that moment, as I was knelt down with tears streaming down my face, I began to feel God's heartbeat. I could feel the loud echo and base of God's heart almost as if it was pounding out of my chest. My heart began to beat rapidly. It was the most remarkable, satisfying and glorious encounter. I wanted time to freeze at that moment. I wanted to savor His heartbeat. I was feeling His Presence in a way that I had never felt before. It was during this time that Chris Caine came up on stage for a brief moment to share about God's heart. She said when our hearts begin to beat for what His heart beats for, this completely changes everything! As we entered back into worship, my heart just kept singing, "Help the mommies and babies, help the mommies and babies. You can help the mommies and babies!" This began a love encounter that only God could have birthed inside not only one heart, but two at the same time.

Since the very first *Embrace Grace* class, the love in our hearts has expanded more and more with each girl who has been a part. We love being able to love and embrace them and their babies. Just as I wondered when I had my firstborn son—*How could I possibly love another baby any more than I love my first?*—I wonder the same with each new class. Then that love miraculously grows, spreads and expands inside of my heart. God grows your heart and expands the love inside of you. Whether you have one child or a hundred and one, every heart touches your life and leaves a lasting impression on you. You desire to see them grow and learn and love like Jesus loves. That is my heart's desire for you. As you read this book, may the love that you feel toward your baby and for Jesus grow more and more each and every day. His love surrounds you. He holds you and comforts you. May you feel His loving arms wrap around you. May you be able to say, "*I am embraced by grace!*"

I will comfort you … as a mother comforts her child. Isaiah 66:13

Jacqueline's Heartbeat

I grew up in a single-parent home. My mom poured her heart and soul into raising my brother and me. I had a happy childhood and remained content with life throughout my teen years. I never knew I had allowed a hole to grow within my heart during my upbringing—a hole longing for the love and approval of a man. I never discovered this, because I was too shy to even talk to boys until I was almost finished with high school.

When I was 19 and entering my second year of college, I naively engaged in a toxic relationship with a man almost a decade older than me. From driven, determined and headed for a college degree, to mentally abused, brain washed and pregnant within three short months, my life took a drastic turn. For a few months I tried daily to convince myself that life would turn out like a dream, anyway, but this man was far from prince charming. And I was beginning to see no matter what expectations of his I strived to meet, he was not going to love or respect me or care about my dreams; but I thought I needed him to be okay having an unplanned pregnancy, to be okay having a baby so young, to be okay with the person I had become. I justified my choices, because I prided myself on having grace for any and everyone, no matter what they had done in their past.

My mother had my best interest at heart no matter the decisions I was making, and informed me shortly into this pretend life I was living, this man had gotten in much bigger trouble in his past than I was led to believe—he was a registered sex offender, whose offenses were against young teenage girls. My whole life I had been told how young for my age I looked, so I knew I was simply "legal" prey for a predator. But even in the midst of my personal downward spiral, God's hand was upon my life and the life of my unborn daughter.

The day my sweet, six-pound little love, Brinley, was born, was a day of transformation and an investing of my heart in a way I had never known. I embraced the responsibility I had for this precious baby, and felt honored to be given a gift so fragile. We moved with my mother into a home she bought, in a city farther from the man who broke my heart, and I was invited to a church that introduced me to true love from a man strong enough to restore my hurting heart. Jesus restored my dreams and gave me new ones; He mended the hole from an absent father, and filled the void of love I had longed for from a man for so long. Each week I would take my baby girl to childcare at church and sit alone in the Saturday night service; it was my "date night with Jesus."

God still has a beautiful life story and love story written

I found myself in a whirlwind of healing, redemption and beautiful romance with the Savior of the world. While wrapped up in His beauty and the new life He'd given me, I was introduced to one of the youth ministers at the church. He led the youth service for teens from single parent homes. He began to pursue me in a way that resembled Jesus' love for me. He did not care to change me or question the choices that brought my daughter into this world. He even told me shortly after we began dating that if I never told him how she came to be, he would still love me and love her, because he loved who God had called us to be.

After six weeks of dating, he took me to the exact place he accepted Jesus into his heart. It was the place he made the first biggest decision of his life, to open his heart to Jesus, and it is where he wanted to make the second biggest decision of opening his heart to me. With my daughter in his arms, he knelt down on one knee and asked me to marry him. He had a new Bible for me, with the most beautiful ring tied to the ribbon inside, and a new children's

Bible for Brinley with a promise as her daddy to always care for and love her.

We were married six months to the day after our first date. And within six months of marriage, we embarked upon the journey for him to adopt Brinley as his own. She is his legal daughter, with the same last name, and knows no one else as her daddy. We also had another precious daughter together, and are continuing to grow our family. This man inspires me daily to seek the Lord for any answer I need. He urges me to find my identity in who God says I am. He encourages me to chase my dreams.

I hope to encourage young, single, pregnant girls that their dreams are not cut short because they had an unplanned pregnancy and have a child at a young age. God still has a beautiful life story and love story written, no matter the choices we make or how far from Him we feel. If we release control of our lives to Him and embrace the grace He wants to give us, we will discover a life and love like nothing we ever could have imagined.

Introduction

"Today is where your book begins.
The rest is still unwritten." –Natasha Bedingfield

With a little whisper, pages of a book take shape, words give birth to sentences, and a simple breath has soon birthed a book of inspiration. Words, thoughts, impressions, lyrics, scriptures—endless impressions impact your heart, as written words speak to this moment of life. It is on these pages that we will bring recollection and remembrance.

Imagine your heart as a book. If you could open the pages of your heart and read the thousands of words, impressions and emotions etched, penned and imprinted upon them, some would be full of joy, laughter, silly times, happiness and beauty, and others, with sorrow, confusion and pain. Perhaps heartache and harsh words appear upon these pages of your heart; maybe some tear stains, too—some from happy cries and others from moments of sadness. Every memory and detail claiming a place within these pages displays your lifetime to reflect on.

It is from the very page you are on right now, the cursor blinking, waiting to write the next sentence of your story, where your journey begins. While you were in your mother's womb, before you were even born, your life's tale began. Psalm 139 creatively describes how you were beautifully and wonderfully made. You have been hand woven and stitched together in your mother's womb, so has your baby in your womb. Look at how this describes in full detail how you and your baby were uniquely handmade.

God is the one who has woven you together without flaw. He has intentionally chosen every physical feature of your body and placed within you every strength and admirable character trait you possess. Along with your physical being, He has written a plan for your life and given you such traits to fulfill a destiny only you could. No one else could play the role in your life as well as you, and you could not substitute anyone else's role. Excitingly, God has not left you alone to figure out each step in the plan He has crafted for you. He is always with you; whether you have acknowledged His presence or not, He has been with you since the beginning of your creation. He has every day you have lived and every day you will ever live written upon pages of His book for you, which is tucked away safely in His heart.

God longs to draw you closer to Him and will tug at your heart's strings. Just as an antique book was bound together with string, your heart contains so many intricacies, as though it is made up of millions of pages laced together by string. Like a harp has strings from which beautiful melodies echo when plucked by fingertips, you also have a heart-song—a melody that is played from your heart which brings joy to your Father's heart.

Some pages of your heart have been tattered and torn; some have been crumpled up and thrown away. God longs to rewrite the pages of your heart and to compose the new ones. His love song, His melody, His tune comes straight from Heaven, whirling in to mend those tatters and tears, cracks and chips. Listen with your ears; look with your eyes; open up all of your heart. He is whispering all around you: in the sunshine, in your child's smile, in the movements inside your womb, in birds singing—all of creation is speaking His heart's song to you. When you open the eyes of your heart and truly see Him for who He is, your perception and outlook on life change. Are you listening? Do you hear what I hear?

A baby changes everything. Perhaps one of the first single and pregnant mothers recorded in the New Testament was Mary, the mother of Jesus. Let's get a glimpse of her story and take a walk in her shoes. Mary was a virgin, engaged to a man named Joseph. An angel came to

Mary during this time of engagement and told her the Lord was with her. She was confused and disturbed and had trouble understanding what the angel meant. "Don't be afraid, Mary," the angel told her, "for you have found favor with God! You will conceive and give birth to a son, and you will name him Jesus. He will be very great and will be called the Son of the Most High." Mary asked the angel, "But how can this happen? I am a virgin." The angel explained that Mary would become pregnant with a holy child through the work of the Holy Spirit. She would give birth to the Son of God (See Luke 1:26-37).

Can you imagine the scene when the angel appeared and spoke with Mary? She was so young and innocent, just a lowly servant girl. She heard the words spoken by the angel, still with no prediction or understanding of what her pregnancy would bring forth. She did not know how her fiancé would react or how her parents would receive the news. And what about neighbors? What would they think? She probably got some looks, second glances and whispers spoken about her. Many people may have called her terrible names upon hearing of her pregnancy.

Savor the snuggle and cuddle time shared with your baby

God sent an angel to Mary and said, "Do not be afraid." He also says to you, "Daughter, do not be afraid. You are not alone." The angel told Mary she had been chosen to carry God's son. You have been chosen out of all the other mothers in the world to carry this baby in your womb. Mary did not know how it would all look or how it would all work out. You may be feeling the same way. She did not know if her husband would trust her. She did not know if others would accept her. Even her family may have felt hesitant or questioning. She could have had stones thrown at her, because she was not married and stoning a person for such an action was the custom in those days. However, she did not let any of that stop her from becoming the mother of Jesus. She simply said, "Let it be unto me as you have said." She did not have all the answers or a manual showing her each step to take. She had to trust that God would show her the way to go. Just as God led Mary, He will lead you step by step as you walk into motherhood. All you have to do is trust Him.

"There was no room for them in the inn," (Luke 2:7 NKJV). There was nowhere indoors for baby Jesus to be born, so He was born in a stable, with animals all around. It was not an extravagant and luxurious hospital, fully equipped with the best nurses and doctors. It was plain and simple. Imagine the smell from the animals. Neither the smell nor the surroundings stopped Jesus from coming into this world as a tiny baby. His mother wrapped Him in swaddling cloths and laid Him in a manger. Perhaps this mention in the Bible was of the first swaddle blanket. Babies love to be swaddled and wrapped so snugly and tightly, to remind them of their time in your womb. Savor the snuggle and cuddle time shared with your baby as you hold him or her. That time is so precious, so full of love. This love nurtures the bond between both of you from the moment your baby is born and beyond.

You brought me safely from my mother's womb and led me to trust you at my mother's breast. I was thrust into your arms at my birth. You have been my God from the moment I was born. Psalm 22:9-10

Habitation

A Safe Haven for Your Heart to Dwell

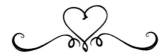

"When I found out I was pregnant, I thought, 'God why are you punishing me?' I was SO ashamed. But over time, I realized that God doesn't hate me; He loves me. And it finally made sense to me—this whole time God's been looking after me, loving me and wanting to have a relationship with me. All I had to do was embrace the grace that was freely given to me."

–Esperanza G.

Haven: any place of shelter and safety

Habitat: a refuge, retreat, shelter, sanctuary, nest, crib

Habitation: a place of residence or home, dwelling, living place, community

God rewrote the text of my life when I opened the book of my heart to his eyes.
Psalm 18:24 The Message

In the book of your heart, you will uncover the pages of your life, including things that have been written and things yet to be written. Healing and restoration are for the taking.

Your heart is the most precious and tender part of your innermost being. This is where you feel love and give love. You cannot give love away freely when you feel empty and have experienced hurt along the way. God wants to fill your heart full and overflowing with love and acceptance. Once you experience God's loving arms and tender embrace, you will see things in a whole new light. A brand-new way of thinking, living and being will intrigue and satisfy you. You will be transformed from the inside out. It is a process that takes time, so please do not try to rush this encounter with God. Everyone learns, grows and reacts in different ways. There are levels and stages to go through. Just as babies learn and develop at their own pace, this will be custom tailored to you. Let's lay aside all comparisons of how others may respond, and receive this gift of unfailing love that is especially for YOU! You will be so thankful that you opened this book and opened up your heart.

Among millions of keys on a key ring, dangles the key to your heart. Jesus holds every key. Like every door has a specific key created to unlock it, your heart claims a special key that has been hand-cut to precisely fit into its lock. In order for us to move forward, you will need to be willing to allow Jesus to show you this handmade key. This is your special key. It has custom-fit ridges and grooves that slide into the lock with ease. No one else has the same key as you. Yours is one of a kind. Are you willing to allow Him to unlock the lock of your heart? He stands knocking. Will you let Him in?

A diary is purposed with a lock on the outside to keep all of your secrets and special treasures, memories and highlights of your days inside. Your heart is purposed with the ability to hold such valuables, as well. All of the pages contained within the diary of your heart hold dreams, hurts, secrets, struggles, weaknesses and so much more. You will not be forced to share your secrets until you are ready. You have a free will and a choice, and it is completely up to you when you open up. Maybe you are unsure or not ready yet, and that is okay. God will wait as long as it takes.

He longs to write upon your heart, and He will offer words specifically for you and where you are in your life at this moment. If you need love, He will bring you words of love. If you need strength, He will bring you words of strength. If you are discouraged, He will bring you words of encouragement. If you need peace, He will bring words of comfort.

Every person has a unique rhythm set to the pace of his or her own life. Place your hand upon your chest and feel your own heart beating. Allow each pulsation to capture the very echo of your life. Your heart is the very special lifeline that keeps you alive. What if you could get a glimpse inside your heart to see every detail of your life it holds? Like a sonogram for your baby, on your heart sonogram what would you be able to see? A lot of joy, happiness, laughter and good times can be seen, but possibly a broken heart, questions about your pregnancy, and emotional wounds, too.

For you are God, my only safe haven. Psalm 43:2

God longs to be a safe place for your heart to dwell, to heal from brokenness, to answer questions and to mend your wounds. He longs to be your safe haven and be invited to inhabit your heart, filling it with love and protection. Whether you live at home with your parents, in your own apartment or have roommates, the place you call home is yours. It is your nest. You have decorated your room or home with your style and flair. You have an area for your baby to lay and play. This is your space—your habitat. You possess the right to invite or allow visitors into your habitat: your home. In the same way, you have the option of opening the door of your heart to Jesus and granting Him access to everything it holds.

Behold I stand at the door and knock; if anyone hears and listens to and heeds My voice and opens the door, I will come into him. Revelation 3:20 NASB

Maybe you have known Jesus for a long time and you are certain of His voice. He is not a stranger to you, but a welcome guest in your heart and home. Perhaps you grew up in church and have heard of Him for years. This could be your first encounter with Jesus. No matter your past, He is standing at the door of your heart and the choice is yours to decide whether He may visit, or make your heart His home. Once you have allowed Him into your heart, you can begin a personal relationship with Him. Jesus came to earth for you, to know you and love you. He saw you when you were far away from Him, troubled and lost, and He loved you still. He paid the ultimate price of sacrifice when He died on the cross to keep you from paying the price of your own failures. Even if there were not another person on earth, He still would have died to save just you. Your one life is so precious to Him. His redemption is for you. All you have to do is believe in Him and ask Him to come and live inside of your heart.

Salvation is a gift that you can freely receive. There is nothing you have to do to earn it. It is freely given, and you only have to open your heart to receive this gift.

For God says, "At just the right time, I heard you. On the day of salvation, I helped you." Indeed, the "right time" is now. Today is the day of salvation. 2 Corinthians 6:2

Then Christ will make his home in your hearts as you trust in him ... Ephesians 3:17

We live in a broken world, with broken, hard hearts, hearts of stone, hearts full of wounds. Even walls built like a fortress are only guarding a hollow heart, empty and missing something. There is a void you can try to fill with addictions such as sweets, guys, sex, drugs, alcohol, smoking, partying, shopping or anything else that brings you temporary satisfaction. But those are all fake fillers. The hole in your heart, that thing you are lacking, can only be completely filled and made whole by Jesus. He is the one true and sure thing that will complete you. He longs to hear you say, "You complete me!"

While there are scars in every heart, they can express hope and represent a beautiful transformation. When we find our safe place in God and know He is holding our hearts and world in the palm of His mighty, gentle, loving hand, we are capable of being vulnerable and open for the world to see our light shine in the way that He has created us to shine, scars included. Hurts, offenses and heartaches cause us to "band-aid" our hearts, build walls, cultivate bitterness, etc. ... so when our hearts beat, they don't beat freely. They thud against those walls of stone that hold them in a place of brokenness and pain, or in patterns of a lifestyle we wish we could be free from.

When we seek a safe place in God and allow Him to chisel away at the walls we've built, to remove our band-aids and temporary fixes and expose our wounds for all they are, no matter how painful or ugly, we give the only one who has the potential to save us the delight to rescue, repair and rebuild our hearts. He gently mends the cuts and tears that rejection, pain and heartache have caused. He replaces temporary bandages and fake remedies with lasting healing and wholeness. He lays a foundation, revealing sacrifice through Jesus' trust and love for us. He gives us an eternal love, with unconditional acceptance. He gives us a hope for joy, peace and dreams galore. Our happily ever after begins with handing over the key to our trapped hearts.

Sometimes we have to dig very deep within our darkest places to find that key and hand it over, but after all of our junk is revealed, He can replace it with treasure and love. Our hearts beat for what His heart beats for. We desire God's heart as we enter the heart transformation program.

And I will give you a new heart, and I will put a new spirit in you. I will take out your stony, stubborn heart and give you a tender, responsive heart. Ezekiel 36:26

"I thought when I first found out I was pregnant that everything was going to go downhill fast, and God has continuously been there for me, providing paths and opening doors."
–Alexandria B.

If you are ready to receive Christ as your personal Lord and Savior and receive this free gift offered, pray the prayer below.

Salvation prayer: *Jesus, I ask You to come and live in me. I realize that I'm empty inside and Your Spirit is not in me. I no longer want to live a life separate from You. I give You my heart and my life. I believe that You died to save me. I ask You to take my key and open the door to my heart and make Yourself welcome. Make my heart Your home. Come and bring healing to the broken places of my heart. I find my safe haven in You. In Jesus' name. Amen.*

When you pray a prayer like that and mean it in your heart, God places His Spirit inside of you and makes you a new creation! God also asks us to confess with our mouths that Jesus is Lord.

Everyone who acknowledges me publicly here on earth, I will also acknowledge before my Father in heaven. But everyone who denies me here on earth, I will also deny before my Father in heaven. Matthew 10:32-33

If any of you pray this prayer, go tell one of your leaders! They will be rejoicing with the angels and will be thrilled!

Action:

Have you asked God into your heart? Where and when did this happen? If you are unsure, you can do this right now or at any time.

....
....
....
....
....
....
....
....
....
....

Will you allow God access to heal your buried pain and past hurts?

....
....
....
....
....
....
....
....
....
....

Mommy's Heartbeat:

When and where did you find out you were pregnant? How did you feel the moment you found out?

....

....

....

....

....

....

....

....

....

....

....

....

....

....

....

....

....

....

....

....

....

....

....

Baby's Heartbeat:

How did you feel during your first ultrasound? What features of your tiny baby could you see?

....
....
....
....
....
....
....
....
....
....

Do you have a strong feeling about whether your baby is a boy or a girl?

....
....
....
....
....
....
....
....
....
....

What hurts and pains have caused you to build up walls around your heart?

Realization

Releasing Doubt and Embracing the Real Deal

"God has impacted my life in so many ways! He not only helped me with the all the negative thoughts going through my head about not going through with this pregnancy and feeling like I deserved a horrible life, but replaced those feelings with so much hope and peace. God's love is overwhelming. I don't have those negative thoughts anymore! I can't even express how much I looked forward to Embrace Grace each week and the urge to hear God's Word and be around all the love with my new friends." –Danielle E.

Real: to be true, existing, actual rather than imaginary, being an actual thing
Realize: to grasp or understand clearly
Realization: the making or being made real of something imagined or planned

The opposite of realization is vacillation, which means to waver in mind or opinion, hesitation—to doubt. Doubt arises in many shapes, forms and fashions. Sometimes it is even in disguise, hidden so we mistake the doubt for truth. When faced with doubts, fears, insecurities and uncertainties, you are robbed of joy and peace. You may constantly worry and question the future. *Can I make it through this situation on my own? What will tomorrow look like? What will happen if...?*

Then you will experience God's peace, which exceeds anything we can understand. His peace will guard your hearts and minds as you live in Christ Jesus. Philippians 4:7

When you put batteries in a toy or an electronic device, you'll find a display showing which direction to insert the batteries. If you put them in incorrectly, what happens? Nothing, right? The power will not turn on. The positive and negative sides of a battery were created with purpose. The same is true with your thought patterns. When we feed and fuel our minds with negative thoughts and doubts, our outlook on life and daily circumstances can look hopeless. If, however, we learn to fill our minds with positive thoughts, our outlook can become exponentially more hopeful.

God has the ultimate controller and solution for your life

When you solely focus on the doubt and fear consuming your mind, your life reflects the uncertainty in your thoughts; what could have been a good life begins to look troubling. Like watching a storm roll in from afar, its dark clouds swallowing a bright blue sky, negativity rapidly overtakes the positivity in all of the dreams you have for your life.

The enemy has a target, and his aim is to get us to fear the unknown and the what if scenarios. If the devil can get us to focus on the negative aspects of our circumstances and become fearful, instead of turning our focus toward God, he feels that he is winning. But God has already won the battle, hands down, so why do we continue to cave in to the devil's pressure and fear the things that are beyond our control?

Fear has been in our nature since birth. Just as an infant hears a loud startling noise and flinches or cries, we instinctively acknowledge fear and react fearfully. There were times when I was pregnant and would soak in the bathtub and my baby would do somersaults inside my tummy. He loved bath time as much as I did. He must have felt me relaxing, but every time I would pull the drain to let out the water, he would jump and then be so still, like he was startled and fearful of the noise from the drain. After a few minutes of calm, he would wiggle and move again. I did not teach him to become unsettled, just as your parents did not have to teach you to become startled or afraid. Maybe you had a fear of the dark or of being alone in a room. These are fears that came at an early age, and the root of that fear came from the enemy—the devil. He desires for us to be shaking in our boots, afraid to open our eyes and see the truth and destiny God has placed within and before us.

It is natural and understandable to have concerns and questions about your pregnancy and your baby. Thinking through the delivery, the pushing or the pain of recovery from a C-Section is normal. Only when these thoughts cause fear and anxiety are they unhealthy to think about. God is the one who can take our fears and calm our tears. He says, "No more worries or fears; no more tears."

My little boy and I were in our hot tub one afternoon, having fun and laughing. All of a sudden the water began to drain quickly from the hot tub and the jets were spewing and splashing water all around. The waves in the hot tub began to feel like a storm for my little boy. My heart felt some confusion of how to explain to him what was happening. As the water crashed on us, my son began to panic, until he remembered a Bible story he had heard at church and excitedly called out, "Jesus, calm the storm!" The moment the words came out of his mouth, the waves settled and the water began to rise back to normal. Around us, the surface of the water grew still and the mini-storm was calmed as quickly as it began. He looked around and said, "Wow, Jesus calmed the storm, Mommy." I smiled at him with a reassuring, "Yes, baby, He sure did."

As I looked to the side of our home, I saw my husband standing with the pool controller in hand. He had simply pushed the button for the water pressure to stop draining, rise again and pump freely throughout the pool and hot tub. Just as easy as it was for him to push that button on the controller, God has the ultimate controller and solution for your life. As soon as you realize He is holding your world, including your storm, in the palm of His hand, you have acknowledged that He also holds the power to walk you through this storm, or calm it altogether.

Storms of life come in many forms. Sometimes the winds and waves can overwhelm you—one huge wave after another. Maybe your storm is in the form of bills, not having a boyfriend, not having a job, having an unplanned pregnancy—a crisis that feels out of control. Sometimes it is hard to see the horizon and shoreline for all the tumultuous waves overwhelming you. There is a similar story in the Bible about a storm that arose when Jesus' disciples were out on a boat in the middle of the water. It was dark, with intimidating clouds looming overhead, and the end of the storm was nowhere in sight. Only when the disciples realized Jesus had the power to calm this storm were they comforted and confident in reaching their destination.

For God has not given us a spirit of fear, but of power and of love and of a sound mind.
2 Timothy 1:7 NKJV

Upon finding yourself in a situation that leaves you feeling out of control, like having an unplanned pregnancy, it can be difficult to prevent anxiety from overtaking your mind, lifestyle and decisions. Within the same few minutes it takes for a pregnancy test to indicate, "pregnant," countless unknowns about your future arise. Every semester we have a new set of *Embrace Grace* girls who come to class for the first time with the same look on their faces: FEAR. You can see it in their eyes, some more than others. *How will I provide for my baby? How will I finish school? How will I find childcare I can afford? What will happen with the baby's father? Should I choose adoption? Will I be a good mom?* Fear-related questions are endless and easily eclipse thoughts of anything else, if you allow them such power over you; so how can you just STOP having fear? Wishing it away seems hopeless, and forcing your thoughts onto other things is only a temporary fix.

When fear is crashing in on you and you find yourself treading water with waves over your head, Jesus says, "Take my hand, and we can make it through this together." When storm clouds are raging all around, Jesus will bring the calm in the middle of the storm and you will be able to breathe easier as the storm passes. He will bring you peace. You are not alone. If the only strength you can muster in the midst of your storm is to say "peace," or speak His name, *Jesus*, over and over again, that is more than enough to bring hope to your situation. In order to release your fear and doubt, you must be willing to open your eyes amidst the swelling waves. When you do, you will realize His hand was reaching for you the whole time, longing to pull you safely ashore. His heartbeat is for you to see how great His love is for you, and how He is waiting for you to allow Him to come to your rescue in this time of uncertainty and doubt.

I recently saw a billboard for a health insurance provider. It read, "When you think about it, there's really not anything to think about." We spend too much time overthinking our circumstances. We choose to dwell on the *what ifs*, obsessing over our situation. But in actuality, are fretting and worrying going to bring change for the better? I am going to venture out and say a resounding, "No." However, if there were a way to stop thinking about all of the doubts and fears you have for your life, your baby's life, your unplanned pregnancy, would you want to know how?

To renew your mind and begin to think positively, you can begin by opening the Bible. Allow God's Word to speak to you and turn your *how, what, when, where* and *why* questions into answers, from the pages of this book full of love and instruction for life. God is the only One who has perfect love for us. Do you KNOW that God loves you? When you finally realize and accept His love—not just with your head, but with your heart, too—the way you think and live changes entirely. Everything you fear melts away when you understand how much you are loved, that God is for you, He has plans for you, He created you for a good purpose, that you are chosen and highly favored.

There is no fear in love; but perfect love casts out fear... 1 John 4:18 NASB

Prayer: *God, I need you—every minute, every hour, every day. Please calm my fear and doubt. Replace them with encouragement and hope. Send Your kisses from Heaven to me each day, and open my eyes and heart to realize how great Your love is for my baby and me. You hold us safely within the palm of Your hands, and You will walk us through every storm we face. Thank You for Your love and protection.*

Action:

After learning about the need to release doubt and embrace God's truth, what encouragement or insight have you gained about realizing He loves you and has a good plan for your life?

....

....

....

....

....

....

....

....

....

....

How can you apply the information from this chapter to your life daily? (Reading your Bible, focusing on the positive, asking God to encourage you, posting encouraging verses around your home, etc.)

....

....

....

....

....

....

....

....

....

....

Mommy's Heartbeat:

How did you feel when you heard your baby's heartbeat for the first time? Who was the first person you told, and what was their reaction?

Baby's Heartbeat:

Who do you think the baby will look most like?

....
....
....
....
....
....
....
....
....
....
....

What physical characteristics do you hope your baby will have?

....
....
....
....
....
....
....
....
....
....
....

HEART CHECK:

What fears and worries do you hide in your heart about your circumstances? What doubts do you have about God in Heaven?

Perception

Seeing with Clarity

"I was given grace and the beginning of something new that made life so much better than it was before. At the time, when I thought so much was wrong with me, the only thing I knew to do was to throw myself into God's arms, and He loved me even more. He was the only one that was going to get me through this and see the light. I just needed to be with Him." –Liz C.

Perception: an intuitive recognition, intuition or apprehension of the mind

Perceptions can be made with first glances, impressions, thoughts, opinions—and may even turn into judgments. We make perceptions by absorbing the world around us through our five senses: sight, sound, smell, taste and touch. With our eyes we see what is out in front of us, whether it's images, objects, pictures, people or sights. Our eyes are the natural perception receptors. With our sight we pick up on colors, hues, light and more. Our other four senses are made to compensate for the loss of eyesight, to capture the setting and your surroundings. Perceptions can be broken down into four different categories: how we see ourselves, how others see us, how we see others and how we see God and Jesus.

Perceptions of ourselves include our identity. We all have one or more attributes we desire to change about ourselves. Some of us even have a list of changes we would like to make to ourselves. One day a friend of mine wonderfully illustrated how we sometimes view ourselves as having flashing, neon signs strapped across our chests. Regardless of whether it is day or night, our signs keep flashing. Maybe your neon sign is flashing, "Insecure." You may feel insecure with your surroundings and not able to walk in the fullness of how you were uniquely created. Maybe your neon sign is flashing, "Unworthy." You may feel unworthy because you are bogged down with shame, guilt or condemnation. Maybe your sign says, "Lost." You may be searching to find out who you really are, unsure of how to discover your identity.

These are only a few examples of what we may be falsely placing upon ourselves. God desires for us to trust Him and believe He is good. He does not want us to question Him, wondering why we have been created with the body, mind and traits that we possess. He created you perfect in His eyes!

Psalm 139 says that God formed our innermost parts in our mother's womb. He knew us before He formed us. When we question what God formed us for, what direction to choose in life or why He made us so different than others, He is waiting to answer our questions and bring clarity to our skewed perception of ourselves. When He gives us insight about how He created us and what purposes we are destined for, we should write it down, so His vision for our lives is available for us to reflect upon when we question our circumstances or life in general.

God sees each of us as lovely. He sees every one of us as a priceless treasure. We are each His precious creation. We must grasp and trust that when God formed our being, He did not make a mistake. In learning to like who we are, there are so many times we focus on what we are not good at. God is strategic and always with purpose. He knew the time every person should be born, and has planned the timing of each baby's birth. He chose you to be this child's mother for such a time as this. He placed everything inside of you that you will need to be the best mommy that you can be.

So many times we sell ourselves short. We think less of ourselves than who we were created to be. It is time to unplug those neon signs draped across our bodies, and throw the brightly-colored labels out with the trash. Those labels do not define who we are. It is time we see ourselves as more valuable and capable than we thought possible. It is time to lay down the guilt, shame, insecurities and anything else that we dislike about ourselves, and learn to love every detail of how we have been created. There is an identity thief on the loose. He is known as the enemy, and he has set out to steal our identities. We must be aware of his mission and intentionally choose to love and own who we are, refusing to exchange ourselves for the counterfeits he offers.

Some of us strive for perfection, always wanting everything around us perfect, including ourselves. We often set our expectations unrealistically high or unbelievably low. As children we may have been pressured to perform without fault or never expected to succeed at all. God has created us just the way He wants us to be. We are made perfect through our failures and imperfections. It is through trial and error we learn from our mistakes and develop character to make better choices in the future, to fully step into the perfect creations He has destined us to become.

Shame is anything that causes embarrassment, dishonor or guilt. It is also referred to as disgrace, which is the absence of grace, the loss of or damage to one's reputation. Shame keeps us from hearing the heartbeat of Heaven for our lives and blinds us from seeing God's vision for our destinies. Shame belittles us into hiding and keeps others from seeing who we really are. Just as sunglasses block the sunlight from hurting our eyes, shame can block the *Son*-shine of Jesus from shining into our lives and encouraging our dreams.

We may hide behind the dark shades hoping no one will see our eyes and how much we are truly hurting. The shades help hide tears and puffy eyes when we have been crying. We may have gone through something as children, as teenagers or recently, tempting us to hide behind a front because we are embarrassed about our actions and afraid of being vulnerable. Jesus wants us to know He doesn't look at us the way we see ourselves. He sees beauty, honor and respect when He looks at us, and He desires for us to behold these great qualities in ourselves, as well. We all have regrets and choices in our past we wish we could take back; however, yesterday is the past, today is a gift and tomorrow is the future. Let's live for today. Let's take off our shades and lose the shame. God is waiting to surround us with His love—over, underneath and all around.

May the Lord bless you and protect you. May the Lord smile on you and be gracious to you. May the Lord show you his favor and give you his peace. Numbers 6:24-26

I have watched the sky and seen the white trails of an airplane or jet gliding across, leaving marks of their flight in the sky. Like a vapor, the plane is here and then gone quickly. Like an eraser brushing across a chalkboard, clearing it of mars and marks, let all past mistakes be wiped away. Picture them vanishing. We are given a clean slate to be ourselves.

"We all find our identity in Christ, but we are all unique. You are so special to God. Only you are purposed for the things God has designed for you to say, do or be. But it all starts with our willingness to turn and embrace Him. To really understand and grasp His great love for you and me." (God Crazy by Michelle Borquez)

When we walk in a room, we sometimes feel as if everyone is looking right at us. Sometimes they are—all eyes on us. And it is not just because of a child within our womb. We carry a glow around and within us. This natural glow brings radiance and light to otherwise dark rooms. Others are drawn to this light, like flowers drawn to sunlight. We must learn to embrace this quality in ourselves and not spin our wheels, wondering what others are thinking of us. For those people out there looking at us and making judgments or accusations, let's try something. Let's choose to bless them. Instead of looking back at them and thinking the worst or being appalled at their thoughts about us, let's choose to bless and not curse them. We will feel encouraged and surprised by choosing to do the right thing, and maybe we can encourage them to do the same.

"I had a really difficult time with judgment. I tried to act like I didn't mind what people thought of me, but the looks and whispers I got on a daily basis cut me so deep. I felt so dirty and ashamed. I'm so thankful to say that my church was the one place I could go and receive no judgment. Instead, strangers would touch my belly and ask what I was having. They would tell me how beautiful I looked or ask me questions about the baby and how I was. To me that was crazy. I had obviously done some not good things, and all they saw was me; not my sin, but me. I wanted to be at church every minute because of the positive environment." –Olivia B.

When in an environment where people are making perceptions and judgments about a young-looking pregnant girl, questioning, *"Is she pregnant? Oh she looks pregnant to me. I wonder how old she is? Did she not now about protection or abstinence? What did her parents think?"*—on and on the list goes—she can respond with an attitude of blessing, for they do not know who this girl really is or anything about her or her situation. She chose life. She is full of life. She chooses to bless them and not hold anything against them for their accusations. We must do the same.

Judgments and deceived perceptions also affect the way we view other people. Comparisons run rampant with our thought life, causing us to feel as if we cannot measure up to the looks, smarts or success of other people. We become certain the grass truly is greener in someone else's yard, and if we could just achieve a hint of what they possess, our grass would turn just as green or greener. If only we could grasp that we are created to be someone entirely different than our neighbors and marvel in our uniqueness, instead of wallowing in our need to blend in with those who appear to have it all together. If only we could learn to be comfortable in our own skin and stop comparing ourselves to other people, and grasp the beauty in differences.

God has a plan for our lives beginning right where we stand

The struggle lies deep within our hearts. The thought of not measuring up or never being enough projects us into a pattern of looking to fill our shoes with someone else's feet. If we can learn to place our feet in the shoes that only we were intended to wear, we would not be met with the great disappointment from failing to succeed at someone else's calling. We spend too much time sorting out thoughts of comparison, when we should be focusing on acts of compassion. When we see another in the midst of a difficulty, we should have a heart of compassion extended to them and offering encouragement and assistance however we can. We must be secure in our places in life, knowing God has put us here to take us to our destinies, so that we can encourage others to become secure in their placement to move onward toward achieving their dreams, as well.

Knowing that God has a plan for our lives beginning right where we stand, we must not have a tainted perception of Him. Our view of Jesus must be free from outside influence.

Jesus walked the earth with a heart full of compassion. His feet went many places. He was on earth for 33 years. Imagine the places His feet walked, the people He touched, healed and blessed, and all the children who climbed into His lap just to be close to Him. He used to be just like them, as He started out His life on earth as a baby. He was a newborn with tiny feet who had to learn how to crawl, take baby steps, walk and run, just like us. Our view of Jesus must perceive His selfless, loving nature and understand He only wants good for us. He would walk millions of miles just to be with us. His time here on earth was short, but His time in Heaven is eternal. He is always here with us. His footsteps are right beside ours, sometimes carrying us when we are too weak to carry ourselves.

When I was younger my family took a trip to Carlsbad Caverns. We had walked for what seemed like miles and miles, or at least that's what it felt like to a 3 year old with short, little legs. My tiny feet were going up and down the many pathways in the caves underground, until suddenly, I realized I could not take another step. I stopped moving my feet and stood still. Right then my Papa reached down, picked me up and placed me on his shoulders. I could go on forever then, because I was not doing the walking myself. Jesus will do the same for you if you let Him. He will carry you through your most difficult days.

Maybe now is the time to lift up your hands in surrender and ask Jesus to pick you up and carry you a while. He is strong enough and big enough. No matter what you are going through, He will carry you. He will show you how to take baby steps into the unknown. He will guide you along the way. He has the best map and the best route. His path is always sure, and His GPS never fails.

I will instruct you and teach you in the way you should go; I will counsel you with My eye upon you. Psalm 32:8 NASB

Jesus is commonly viewed as being distant or very strict. Many believe He expects too much perfection. But none of these views are true. Maybe we are looking through the lens or a pair of eyes that display a fuzzy view. Just as words appear fuzzy and distorted for a nearsighted or farsighted person without their glasses on, we may have distorted perceptions of God and Jesus. When we see with clarity, we behold His grace, mercy, truth and unconditional love.

Your word is a lamp to my feet and a light to my path. Psalm 119:105 NASB

"My beautiful baby girl was born on October 8th, 2011 at 2:13 in the afternoon. I remember that moment, because that is when my life truly began. I had a reason for living, a life to guide and protect. All of the pain that had happened over the past year completely vanished. She was my little miracle. This tiny life saved mine. I honestly believe that if it was not for her, I would be dead somewhere or living in complete numbness. My unplanned pregnancy turned my life around completely. God used this "mistake" to bring me back to Him and to be a light for others." –Devin S.

Prayer: *God, thank You for the gift and calling of motherhood. Help me to remember that my love for my children is merely a reflection of Your own love for them. With that in mind, give me grace to surrender my anxiety. Replace it with a sense of trust and calm as I learn to depend on You for everything. Help me take the blinders off and help me to see myself and others the way You see us. I need You to pick me up and carry me a while so I can rest in Your grace and love. Amen.*

Action:

How has your view of God and Jesus changed as you have discovered a new perception of His heart for you?

....
....
....
....
....
....
....
....
....
....

When overwhelmed with how other people seem to have the "perfect" life, what can you replace your thoughts of comparison with?

....
....
....
....
....
....
....
....
....
....

Mommy's Heartbeat:

What is your biggest fear about your pregnancy, and what is your biggest hope?

....

....

....

....

....

....

....

....

....

....

....

....

....

....

....

....

....

....

....

....

....

....

....

....

Baby's Heartbeat:

What are some of your choices for baby names?

....
....
....
....
....
....
....
....
....
....
....

Have you looked up the meaning of any names you have chosen?

....
....
....
....
....
....
....
....
....
....
....

HEART CHECK:

In what ways have you previously tried to change yourself, but now embrace the uniqueness in who you are and how God created you?

Expectation

Embracing Faith and Trust

"I have finally begun to see just how much God loves ME! I realize now that His relationship with me is based on His love for me, and not how well I measure up." –Audra F.

Expectation: the act of expecting or to wait in expectation, as in expecting a baby
Anticipation: awaiting, high hopes, looking forward, notion, promise, trust
Faith: confidence or trust in a person or thing, belief in God
Trust: a confident expectation of something, hope, to believe, sureness

Excitement builds inside when we await something hoped for. When expecting a baby, the mother is due to experience a miracle. She has a beating heart of a little life growing inside of her womb. With pregnancy comes many expectations, hopes or hope nots.

When you climb onto a rollercoaster, you know that very first drop is ahead, and you are locked in. You have counted the clicks as the cars cranked higher and higher. You have a preconceived idea of what lies before you. Excited, terrified, heart pounding and short of breath, you are ready to scream and cannot wait, but don't want it to happen either. Torn between hoping that drop never comes, while also hoping it hurries up, emotions whirl inside your mind.

When you found out you were pregnant, similar feelings might have overwhelmed you. A baby is so small, yet intense fear and questions can consume a mommy's heart. But all of the sweet possibilities of what this little baby will look like, if it is a boy or a girl, what name will you choose and other positive possibilities mix excitement with the fear. A baby changes everything.

Amy and I attended a Carnival at Gateway, and I begged her to go on the Skymaster with me. It was like a topsy-turvy ride. You buckle your seatbelt and strap in, because when the ride begins, there is no stopping it. You hang upside down and are suspended in the air. It just flips over and over again. It is a wild ride! God is your Skymaster. He will take you on incredible rides. You will have the time of your life, just as Amy and I are having on this wild ride together with God and *Embrace Grace*. He is always surprising us, bringing favor above and beyond what we could have ever asked, dreamed or imagined. She will call or text and say, "Guess what?" And the expectation in my heart is always ready for more!

Preparation is evidence of expectation. You have been coming to class each week, preparing your heart to listen and receive all that God has for you. You have been in preparation for your baby to arrive and going through the nesting stages. You are prepared to be the mommy that God has called you to be! He will lead you along the way, every step and in every way … all the way!

The Word of God is like a tiny seed, full of life, which will grow naturally in our hearts.

In the beginning was the Word, and the Word was with God, and the Word was God. John 1:1 NASB

'The word is near you, in your mouth and in your heart.' –that is, the word of faith which we are preaching. Romans 10:8 NASB

A farmer waits in expectation as he prepares his garden or field. He has plowed and cultivated the land. Seeds have been planted. He waits with anticipation for the rain to come. The sun shines down and brings the warmth, vitamins and nutrients needed for roots to grow deep down. He looks intently at the land, awaiting any sprouts rising from the soil. He has faith that his field will produce an abundant harvest.

Our hearts are the soil, and the seeds are planted within. The enemy believes he has triumphed, because he does not see any growth for a while. The evidence is tucked under the dirt. He sees no evidence of sprouting. But soon, the bud is blossoming and blooming. There will be an overflow in our hearts. We will see the fruit bursting forth: heart rhythm— new hearts that beat with your heart. –Pink Impact 2012

As the farmer sees the harvest his preparation has produced, you will also see great favor and blessings sprout in your life because you have prepared your heart, like the farmer prepared his soil. You have opened it up to God and allowed Him to clear out the past weeds and make you whole, new and prepared for life with Him and life with your baby. Or if you have chosen adoption, He has cleared your past weeds and made you whole and new and prepared the family you are blessing your baby with, while He also prepares you for your future dreams.

"Sometimes in the hard stuff, there is good stuff, too. You've just gotta open your eyes to it. Without the hard stuff, I wouldn't be me. Without the hard stuff, I wouldn't have so much. Without the hard stuff, my life wouldn't be as easy as when I have God. My hope in Jesus is bigger than any circumstance." –Brooke D.

I love pregnant bellies more than anything! I am a baby lover! I am fascinated at how beautiful ladies become as they begin to stretch and grow into their baby bump. From the moment you find out you are pregnant, that tiny baby begins to grow inside of you and a piece of your heart begins to grow along with your baby. This love and bond grow stronger and deeper each and every moment. There are days further along in your pregnancy when you think there is no way your belly can stretch any more, it has reached it's capacity and it could not possibly grow any larger. But amazingly, it does. Just as your tummy begins to stretch with each passing day of your pregnancy, the elasticity of your skin was created to stretch in this fascinating way to allow room for your baby to develop and stay cozily nestled within you.

As surprising as it is to see your tummy begin to stretch and grow with each passing day, you are also being stretched on the inside of your heart. A love for your baby begins to expand your heart, like the bellybands provide more room for your middle as your pants begin to get a little tighter. That bellyband can be a picture of what we as mommies experience. Yes, during pregnancy you stretch and grow and see the results on your belly. After your labor and delivery, your tummy does go down, eventually, and your baby is here on this earth in your care or the care of his or her adoptive family.

Sometimes we have an expectation of what life will be like with a baby; sometimes we have an idea of how we want any given day to go—smoothly, with no surprises or trouble. But when days do not go as planned with our babies, older children or other life demands, we feel stretched further than we could have imagined—emotionally, mentally, maybe even physically, like when our pregnant bellies were growing. When we become accustomed to our comfort zones, predictable routines and what we are used to, change can really disrupt our satisfaction with life. During these times, we must have faith and trust that God is going to pull us through the difficulties and on to a new and brighter day or season of life. We will feel more accomplished, with a greater sense of victory and integrity than we would have had we not gone through a rough patch of time. If we exercise faith during hard times, we will have more strength and stamina during our next bad day.

God wants us to have childlike faith

God will not ask us to be stretched more than what we can handle with Him by our side. He will give us the elasticity, flexibility and adaptability that we need. With each new day, we can rise up and be confident in knowing that God is going to take care of us.

Oh that will be a day … A day for stretching your arms, spreading your wings … Micah 7:11 The Message

We're able to stretch our hands out and receive what we asked for because we're doing what He said, doing what pleases Him. 1 John 3:21 The Message

My little boy asked me one morning while we were driving in the car, "Mommy, are you still growing?" I giggled at the thought of his question. His sweet innocence and childlike perceptions always come with such tenderness. I thought to myself before responding to his question. "Well, sometimes I can see I have eaten a little more than usual and my pants fit a little snugly," but that was not what he was expecting to hear, so I reevaluated.

My new response to his question was simply, "Mommy is growing on the inside, but you are growing daily on the inside and outside. You are only four years old. You can see yourself getting taller and growing bigger every day. Mommy does not grow any taller, but she is always growing on the inside, learning more things, growing closer in her relationship with God and with others. You are growing on the inside, too. When we read our Bible together and you listen to your stories at church, then you are growing and learning good things, too. This helps us to show kindness to one another." He accepted the response, but for months would still ask the same question, wondering with his little childlike eyes.

God wants us to have childlike faith, as if to see the world through a child's eyes. Children do not have the daily pressures of wondering how or what they will eat, what they will wear, what new troubles will pop up tomorrow. They live for today, carefree, and have little concerns. They know they are safely protected and provided for. They know they will be fed, clothed and loved.

Childlike faith is when we can come to God and crawl up in His lap and say, "God, I do not know how all of this is going to work out, but I trust that You know what is best for me. Your timing is always right on time. I trust that you will guide me through each step of the way." Having childlike faith is resting and knowing that all of your needs will be met. That you will be clothed, fed, loved, held, picked up, protected, comforted, nurtured, safe and sound, warm and cozy, have a roof over your head and so much more!

The Lord protects those of childlike faith; I was facing death, and he saved me. Psalm 116:6

"The Lord promises to protect me, the Lord promises to comfort me, the Lord promises to deliver me, the Lord promises to answer me." My son Logan spoke these promises at age 4. We were in the car one day, and he began to tell me how the Lord makes him promises. He says, "You can't see God; He is invisible. I see God when I close my eyes." I asked, "When do you hear God, Logan?" He answered, "When I see ladybugs and butterflies and when I look at you. He whispers to my heart." What a statement of truth about God spoken by a child.

Jesus will not ever walk too far ahead of you or too far behind you. He will be by your side. He wants you to learn how to hear, believe and obey. You may be hearing or reading something in these pages and that particular thing speaks to your heart and you think, *Hey, I was just feeling that same way.* That is Him letting you know you are not alone. You may feel like you are walking this road alone during your pregnancy and single parenting and no one else understands exactly what you are feeling. Tell Him about it. Express your concerns and frustrations. He can take it. He knows and cares so deeply about you. He loves you, and He longs for you to know Him, too.

Faith is like a rubber band; it's only useful when it's S-T-R-E-T-C-H-E-D. The other day I grabbed a huge rubber band from my husband's office drawer. It was the biggest one I could find. I placed it on my arm and kept it as a reminder all day long. God had whispered for me to open the drawer and grab the biggest band I could find. He shared with me that He is going to stretch me beyond what I thought I could ever be stretched. Your faith can expand just as the rubber band, and you will not snap. Even the smallest amount of faith will stretch miles more than you might think.

"You don't have enough faith," Jesus told them. "I tell you the truth, if you had faith even as small as a mustard seed, you could say to this mountain, 'Move from here to there,' and it would move. Nothing would be impossible." Matthew 17:20

Have you ever seen a Green Giant commercial? You know, the Jolly Green Giant who stands in a field of vegetables and at the end of each commercial says, "Ho, ho, ho! Green Giant." Well, I had a dream about that giant. There were mountains all around me in my dream. All of a sudden, the Green Giant focused his eyes up over the mountains, standing taller than any of the mountains that I could see. With his hands upon his hips, wearing green tights and something resembling vegetables as clothing, I saw that he was jolly and funny and made me laugh. He was not intimidating or anything to fear. I woke up thinking about giants that I am facing. *Do I look at them and want to run away in fear? Or do I have the courage to face the giants head on?* I need to have faith that I can face the giant and not fear. We should not tell God how big our mountain is, but instead tell the mountain how **BIG** our God is!

Trust in the Lord with all your heart; do not depend on your own understanding. Proverbs 3:5

And now O Lord what do I wait for and expect? My hope and expectation are in you. Psalm 39:7AMP

But this I recall and therefore I have hope and expectation: It is because of the Lord's mercy and loving-kindness that we are not consumed, because His [tender] compassions fail not. Lamentations 3:21-22 AMP

"This path we are on is the one the Lord set out for us. He is so faithful and amazing. I feel confident and sure that no matter the circumstances or hardships I face, I can always look to God. I can always take His hand, and He will lead me to where I'm meant to be. I have never in my life felt so happy, hopeful or sure that knowing Jesus and seeking Him are exactly what I was made to do. So now, at 22, I lift my heart and my household up to Jesus, and I can honestly say, He has His hand on my son and me." –Dylan D.

Prayer: *God, give me the strength today that I will need to be the mommy that You have created me to be. In all situations, may I look to You as my Source for all things. As I am being stretched, may I embrace the flexibility that You alone can provide me with. Grant me the grace, patience and love to nurture and tend to my little one(s). I love You and thank You for the gift that You have placed within me. Amen.*

Action:

What expectations of yourself do you need to let go of today, so you can think and live freely?

....
....
....
....
....
....
....
....
....
....

Have you ever had a time when something happened and it was better than you expected? If so, what did you expect and how was it better?

....
....
....
....
....
....
....
....
....
....

Mommy's Heartbeat:

Have you had a moment during your pregnancy when you have cried out to God for help, and felt like you so desperately needed Him? Has He been showing you He is there and hears you?

....
....
....
....
....
....
....
....
....
....
....
....
....
....
....
....
....
....
....
....
....

Baby's Heartbeat:

When did you first feel the baby move? Where were you?

November 1st, laying on my stomach, I woke
to the sound of rain on my parents window
the morning of my wedding. Listening to
the water fall from the sky hoping that it
would stop before the ceremony and
I felt John's movements like flutters and
bounces almost a "tapping".

Who was the first person other than you to feel the baby move?

~~My sister and mother~~
Alex, then my sister, then my mother.

HEART CHECK:

In what ways can you trust God and have faith that He will come through for you?

Revelation

Revealing the Lies and Embracing God's Truth

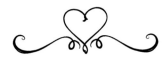

"I had a revelation that God chose me out of all of the girls in the world, to be my son's mom. He made me beautiful, and He would always love me. He filled that hole I had been searching to fill. He blessed me with an amazing child when I finally let Him in my heart."
—Meaghan W.

Revelation: something revealed, to make known, unveiling, the truth
Truth: something true, honest, filled with integrity
Fabrication: something fabricated, false, a lie, deception, deceit, fable, fake, fib, figment of your imagination, untruth

Jesus told him, "I am the way, the truth, and the life ..." John 14:6

So what is the simple truth? The best example in the world of truth is God's Word, the Bible. The Bible is living and active. When I was a little girl, I remember watching a movie called, *The Never-Ending Story*. The stories in the book would come alive, and the reader could reenact the scenes and adventures while reading aloud the words on the pages. It truly was never-ending.

The same is even more true with the Bible. When you begin to read it, the words can come alive and you can feel as if you are part of the story. You can reenact the amazing miracles and scenes from the Old and New Testament. You can fully engage and become part of the stories, too. You can see yourself as the characters that are depicted on the pages. You can close your eyes and imagine the settings and be a part of the story as it unfolds. You can picture yourself as Mary the Mother of Jesus as she had an unplanned pregnancy as a virgin and what feelings she must have felt. Or as the woman at the well who was searching for something or someone to complete her, when suddenly Jesus gave her life meaning and significance. Or Esther as she used her favor with the King to boldly put her life on the line in order to save her people. There are so many amazing and beautiful stories all within the pages of the Bible. When you can step into that moment in time and truly see yourself in those days and then relate it to your modern daily life, it can truly be life changing.

... I lovingly embrace everything you say. Psalm 119:119 The Message

The Bible is so full of truth, wisdom and understanding. The more you read, the more you will begin to hunger for more. "Like newborn babies you should crave [thirst for, earnestly desire] the pure spiritual milk, that by it you may be nurtured and grow unto completed salvation" (1 Peter 2:2 AMP). The pure spiritual milk is the Bible. As you are sitting down to feed your baby their milk, and you are nourishing their body, you too can fill up with spiritual milk as you read the Bible and nourish your soul.

Pray and seek Him with your whole heart!

God's desire is for us to seek Him. The more we seek Him, the more we find Him. We can seek Him by reading His Word. When we begin reading and digging into the scriptures and truth, it will be easier for us to know how to stand. When the enemy tries to lie to us and whisper those thoughts in our minds that we know are not ours or from God, we can begin to quote scriptures, *the simple truth*, and the enemy must flee.

Once you begin to have God's Word in your heart and really believe what He says is true, daily circumstances will not seem so big and impossible because you'll know you can rely on God's promises. You may be having a really rough day—and let's face it, we all have these days from time to time—and you may think it's not ever going to get any better. But then you can remember what you have read, the real and simple truth, and know that you can put your faith and hope in Jesus. He will bring you through whatever you are going through in His timing. It may not be when you think or expect it to happen; only God knows what is best for you!

I love to play hide and seek with my children. We pick favorite hiding spots and sit, waiting for the seeker to come find us. Sometimes they find us quickly. Other times we may be sitting in that same spot for a while, even whistling a happy tune, wondering when they are going to find us. We may even think, *Did they forget about me? Are we still playing the game?*

The suspense in seeking and finding someone brings out the best of the inner kids in us. Everyone wants to be found. Some of you may feel like you have been playing a game of hide and seek for a while. You may feel lost or that people have forgotten about you. Maybe since you have become pregnant, some of your friends have turned their backs on you because you are not able to hang out as much or do the things that you used to always do together. But God isn't hiding from you. He is waiting for you to draw near to Him. He will seek you when you seek Him.

Come close to God, and God will come close to you … James 4:8

Don't just wait until you are going through a hard time in your life, to come close to God. There is more peace in our lives when our thoughts are fixed on our heavenly Father's. Some of the ways you can draw close to Him are by worshipping Him, studying His Word and having daily quiet time with Him. Carve out some time by getting up a little earlier or setting aside time on your lunch break. Schedule it on your calendar if you need to! Pray and seek Him with your whole heart! He will not back off. He will draw close to you when you move toward Him. The closer you are to Him, the more the enemy's lies get drowned out.

Every good thing given and every perfect gift is from above, coming down from the Father of lights … James 1:17 NASB

Satan is constantly lying to you and me. He is trying to bring you into agreement with himself. One of his most effective strategies is to use hurtful words to attack you, and he will use anyone to inflict the pain and hurt on you—a loved one, a parent, a best friend, a baby daddy, family or someone close to you. He can even use strangers to attack you with accusations. Those words are like arrows that pierce your heart to the core. The enemy uses the resulting pain to convince you of his lies and to get you to agree with him about whatever or whoever spoke the hurtful words to you. The wounds can be physical, emotional, spiritual or any combination of the three. It is important to understand that peoples' experiences and emotions are real. These could be memories and hurts that you experienced as a child, as you were growing up or even recently.

… He (Satan) was a murderer from the beginning. He has always hated the truth, because there is no truth in him. When he lies, it is consistent with his character, for he is a liar and the father of lies.
John 8:44

Let's ask God what He wants to say to you. Close your eyes and focus on Him. As you are being still and quiet, He may bring a memory, a picture or a thought to your mind. Maybe something that you experienced that has caused you sorrow and pain. He wants to restore your brokenness and take those hurtful words that were toxic and replace them with His words of love to you that bring life! The only way to replace the lies with the truth is to bring those lies into the light and acknowledge them first.

I believed a lie—_____—and do not accept that in my mind and heart anymore.

I choose to believe the truth—_____

A lie that you could have believed:	The truth to those fabrications:
I am not going to be a good mom.	I am going to be a GREAT mom.
I do not have what it takes.	I DO have what it takes.
I am unqualified.	I AM qualified.
I am too broken.	I AM complete and whole.
I am a failure.	I AM a success.

Used in or paraphrased from Gateway Freedom Ministry

And you will know the truth, and the truth will set you free. John 8:32

But those who do what is right come to the light so others can see that they are doing what God wants. John 3:21

Our words are powerful. We can speak life over ourselves or speak death. Speaking the truth out loud is life to us! Even if you need to write your truths out and put them on your mirror to read as your getting ready, or maybe on your car visor to read through at a red light, put it anywhere throughout your day to remind you of the *truth*. Read the words out loud any time the lies start creeping back in.

Death and life are in the power of the tongue, and those who love it will eat its fruit. Proverbs 18:21 NASB

"I know now I am not a horrible person like I thought I was, and I know now how much God loves me and my baby. I now have the courage to raise my daughter, and I believe I will be a great mom." –Dianna S.

I want to be real, authentic and truthful with you throughout our adventure together. I would like to share with you a lie that I believed for a really long time. It wasn't until recently that I even realized I had bought into and believed the lie. A guest speaker came to our church and spoke to the congregation about how Satan is the "Hurt Whisperer." He whispers hurtful things to us all the time, and sometimes we start believing those lies. Satan is the father of lies.

During that message, God began to reveal things in my heart that I had agreed with but that were not true at all. I allowed God to speak to my heart and further in my journal when I went home that afternoon. I began pouring out my heart in words on the pages. God really spoke to my heart in depth. I sat in a rocking chair and imagined sitting in His lap and He held me as I cried. Suddenly I wrote the word *insignificant*. Then it clicked. A lie that I had believed about myself was that I was insignificant. I felt that I was not good enough or could not finish the task laid out before me. This lie was planted in me at an early age of 6 years old, and it seemed like the lie became almost part of my identity. It was just something that

I always had believed, without even giving much thought as to *why* I believed that lie.

As God was revealing all of this to me, He began to show me pictures of me as a little girl and brought back to my attention *some true* things He had spoken over my life. God had always spoken truth, but soon after, the enemy came and whispered lies and I bought into those lies. I believed things like, *That is not really what you heard. You are just making that up. You can't really think that you can do that. I mean, really? Come on. You are just a little girl. That is not really going to happen. No one is even listening to you.* So I tucked the truths so far down deep into my heart, I forgot all about them … until now!

…Your revelation is the only truth. Psalm 119:142 The Message

I decided I was not going to accept this lie about myself in my mind and heart any longer. I rejected the lie. Then I chose to believe the truth that I *am* significant. And suddenly, it was as if a light bulb appeared right over my head, as if something jumped off the page right at me. That was when I wrote the word *significant*. I looked at that word and began repeating it over to myself. I was making a declaration. I was coming into agreement with the truth. I was lining up my heart with God's and believing His truth about myself. The word then took on a whole new meaning.

Sign-if-i-cant. *It's a sign that if I can't … GOD CAN!* All along I was thinking that these things were so big and enormous and there was no way I could do the things He was asking me to do. I was placing limitations on myself and God, but He was not asking me to do them alone. It's a sign that I can fully surrender and say, "*God, I can't do this on my own. In my own strength I am weak and powerless, and I am nothing without You. God, I know that YOU CAN! You are mighty and powerful and strong enough. You can do all things. Nothing is impossible for You! With You our possibilities are limitless!*"

I can do all things through Christ who strengthens me. Philippians 4:13 NKJV

I cried and said, "*God I am so sorry for believing this lie and I repent. I choose to believe the truth.*" You can do the same! Reject the lies and believe the truth. Don't be intimidated any longer by someone's false words spoken over you. Reject them immediately and do not let them sink into your heart.

"All of these thoughts went through my head as I sat there and listened to my baby's father talk down to me about the pregnancy and how big of a mistake it was. I just sat there, let him go off on me, but when he was done, it was like God lifted me up and spoke for me. I said, 'I am keeping this baby, and there is absolutely nothing you can do or say that will change my mind.'" –Jenn M.

Intimidation is a real trick of the enemy, often disguised in a stranger's voice. It can be in the form of bullying, threatening, even scare tactics. Are you listening to the stranger's voice? Does it sound oppressive, depressive, make you want to throw in the towel or just give up? The enemy wants to torment us, but you don't have to be tormented any longer. The blood of the Lamb was shed for you. You are living and covered by grace and mercy. As we listen for God's voice, we must be able to discern it from other voices.

For God has not given us a spirit of fear and timidity, but of power, love and self-discipline.
2 Timothy 1:7

You can take every thought, dream and word spoken to you captive individually and determine if it's from God, the devil or yourself.

God's voice: loves and encourages us, always speaks positive truth, gently convicts us of our sin and offers forgiveness, never compares, always extends us to do more than what we think we can, wants us to trust Him, gives clear direction and instruction and wants all the honor and praise.

Satan's voice: hates and discourages us, speaks negatively and talks down to us, lies, condemns and shames us for our sins, blames us, rejects us, coerces comparison, tries to convince us that we are not capable of something that we ARE capable of with God, makes us feel insignificant, does not want us to trust God, gives confusing instruction and wants all the honor and praise.

If it's our own thoughts, then we will know because it sounds a lot like, "ME, ME, ME" and "I, I, I." Everything becomes about us. The center of our thoughts have all the focus on ourselves. Maybe it's a manipulative thought, possibly controlling or even materialistic. We see everything around us for what it is, instead of seeing things the way God sees us. We limit ourselves because we put all our trust and hope in our physical abilities and the way our world is right now, instead of putting our faith and trust in God and believing He is going to be there to help us. Oh, and just like God and Satan, we want the honor and praise, too. We have to align our hearts with God's by spending time in His Word and with Him, so that His thoughts become ours.

"My thoughts are nothing like your thoughts," says the Lord. "And my ways are far beyond anything you could imagine. For just as the heavens are higher than the earth, so my ways are higher than your ways and my thoughts higher than your thoughts." Isaiah 55:8-9

So humble yourselves before God. Resist the devil and he will flee from you. James 4:7

- If you recognize a thought that is from Satan, yell out a loud NO and watch him go.
- If you recognize a thought that is your own and not of God, repent and ask for forgiveness for letting your own selfish thoughts interfere with God's plans.
- If you recognize a thought that is from God, say a quiet YES, and He is there to help you and continue to lead.

My sheep [my people] listen to my voice; I know them, and they follow me. John 10:27

The closer we draw to God, the easier it is to recognize His voice when He speaks to our hearts. Let God's Word of truth wash over you and lift you up. God wants us to seek Him daily to guide our path. When I am searching for truth, I can always turn to the *truth* to get answers. Carve out time to read His Word and spend time with Him and watch your life begin to change!

Prayer: *Jesus, uncover the truth. Speak to my heart. Shine Your light into the darkness and reveal the truth of how You see me. Change my heart from the inside out. Change the way I think and help me recognize and reject the thoughts that are not of You. I choose to believe the truth about myself and fill my heart up with spiritual milk as I read Your Word. Reveal Yourself to me as I draw near to You.*

Action:

What scripture or passage of scriptures (truth) have brought a new revelation and changed the way you see yourself by seeing through God's eyes?

....
....
....
....
....
....
....
....
....
....
....

What lies that have been spoken over you or that you have believed about yourself, are you ready to reject?

....
....
....
....
....
....
....
....
....
....
....

Mommy's Heartbeat:

Have you felt God's presence in a new or different way during your pregnancy? Has He been speaking to your heart? How has He shown His love in your life?

....

....

....

....

....

....

....

....

....

....

....

....

....

....

....

....

....

....

....

....

....

....

....

Baby's Heartbeat:

What was the first present you received for the baby? How did it make you feel?

....
....
....
....
....
....
....
....
....
....

What is the first thing you bought for the baby?

....
....
....
....
....
....
....
....
....
....
....
....

HEART CHECK:

After rejecting each lie, what truth(s) are you now accepting, receiving and believing about yourself that lines up with God's *truth(s)?*

Conviction

Resisting Temptation and Embracing God's Purpose

Conviction: a belief, opinion, mind, persuasion, reliance, say so, view

Sin: an act of disobedience, a willful violation, regrettable action

Conscience: one's sense of right and wrong, inner voice, still small voice

Temptation: tempting, enticing, alluring, attraction

Testing: a test, trial, verify or verification

God brings conviction, but never condemnation. Since you have allowed God to come into your life, you may sometimes feel a gentle nudging on your conscience from the Holy Spirit to convict you of sins when decisions are made that do not line up with God's Word. He wants the very best for us and uses the Holy Spirit to speak to and guide us to follow His perfect purpose and awesome destiny He has planned for our lives. He will never condemn us or remind us of our past sins, even after our sins have been forgiven. God does not make us feel unworthy or ashamed. He wants us to draw near to Him with a sincere and open heart.

When we stay aware of our thought patterns and what we allow ourselves to think about, we can easily recognize the difference between Satan's lies and God's thoughts for us. The enemy brings temptation, condemnation and judgment upon us. Condemnation is any form of blame, guilt, accusations, belittling and even feeling like we are being punished. The enemy will use all types of avenues to bring this condemnation against us. He wants to make us feel as down, dirty and as disqualified as he can. He is known as a thief. In John 10:10, it says he is here to kill, steal and destroy us. He thinks if he can keep us down and focused on our pasts, then we will not be able to walk in the joy, confidence and perfect plan that God made for us before we were even born. Do not accept those lies; reject them immediately.

God makes an awesome promise in the second half of John 10:10 that will bring joy to our hearts and a spring to our step. God says, "… *I came that they may have and enjoy life, and have it in abundance (to the full, until it overflows)*" (AMP). That means what the enemy came to steal, kill and destroy, God has come to turn into an abundant life and we no longer have to be burdened down by the sins and weight of this world. We are made righteous, or in right standing with Jesus. He paid the ultimate price for us on the cross. We are no longer bound to the sins of this world! Anything we have ever done in our pasts or will do in our futures has already been paid for. He paid the weight of our sins on the cross, once and for all. There is nothing that we have to do to earn this gift. It is pure redemption. This is a beautiful and free gift that has been given to each of us.

One day when my son Landan was seven years old, we went grocery shopping together. Driving in the car on the way there, I had been praying for wisdom in parenting and discipline. I had no idea that this little bit of wisdom would come so swiftly.

As I was emptying the cart on the counter to check out, the cashier started to ring up our groceries. There was a small line of people forming behind me, waiting for us to finish. Landan looked up at me with his big brown eyes and asked politely, "Mom, can I have this big Hershey's Kiss?" I responded, "Yes you may have that, but please do not eat it until we get home to watch our movie together." He agreed, and I turned to unload more groceries from the cart.

A few moments later I heard, "Mom …" I turned back around to see Landan with his eyes open wide, holding that big Hershey's Kiss in his hand with the wrapper open and a huge bite taken off the top. I said, "Landan! I asked you to wait until we got home to eat the Kiss." He replied, "But mom, it looked so good! I just couldn't resist …" I turned and hurriedly paid for the groceries, and we walked outside together. Landan held on to his Kiss in the palm of his hand all the way home. We walked inside the house. I opened the trashcan and said, "It's time to kiss your Kiss goodbye." He looked at me with his jaw dropped, then down at the trash can, and then back up at me. "Mom, you can't just throw this candy away." He knew I meant business. He literally kissed his big Hershey's Kiss goodbye, took a long look at it and then threw it into the trash. He learned a good lesson of obedience at that moment. In the future, he might feel convicted to obey his parents the first time he's told.

The first man and woman in the Bible, Adam and Eve, learned a similar lesson the hard way. Their story is found in Genesis 3. They lived in a beautiful garden where they were able to walk around freely without any guilt, shame or fear. They were naked and unashamed. They walked with God in the cool of the day in the Garden of Eden without any cares of the world on their shoulders. They were happily content without insecurities or any reason to hide. Everything was peaceful. There was only one tree God told Adam and Eve not to eat from.

One day a serpent spoke to the woman and said, "Did God really say you must not eat from any trees in the garden? You will not surely die. For God knows that when you eat of it, your eyes will be opened and you will be like God, knowing good and evil."

The woman listened and began to allow the serpent's temptation to overtake her thoughts, and she wondered, *Could I really be like God?* She was enticed, gave in to her desire and picked the fruit from the tree. She took a bite from it and shared the fruit with her husband, Adam. Soon after, they heard a voice coming from somewhere in the Garden. They looked around and suddenly realized they were naked. They had lived freely until that moment of disobedience. When sin entered their hearts, they allowed shame to influence them. They hid from God, aware of their disobedience.

The devil wants you to live in a state of condemnation, so he is going to tempt you to sin and make poor choices, just as he tempted Eve to eat the fruit from the only tree God instructed them not to eat from. Once you fall into Satan's temptation and sin, he will use it against you to lock you in a place of defeat, preventing you from discovering the blessings God has for your life. Whereas, when we sin and immediately go to God with our mess-ups, He forgives us without hesitation or condemnation. We are loved as though we never sinned, but we are convicted not to repeat the same mistake again.

And do not lead us into temptation, but deliver us from evil … Matthew 6:13 NKJV

God will not tempt us. It is outside of His nature to do so, but it is Satan's mission to lead us to make poor choices. When we endure temptation and make wise choices, we will be blessed and rewarded.

The most successful way to avoid temptation is to turn our focus toward God. When we are captivated by His love and plan for us, we are less likely to be swayed by other distractions. Our heartbeats align with His heartbeat. His desires become our desires. Attention breeds desire. What we focus our attention on is what we desire.

Dear brothers and sisters, when troubles come your way, consider it an opportunity for great joy. For you know that when your faith is tested, your endurance has a chance to grow. James 1:2-3

When we go through trials, God is shaping and molding us to not only grow our own faith, but to inspire others by our victories. He uses everything we go through as a launching pad to our destiny. Jesus wants to be our best friend and the first person we turn to for help in a time of need or struggle. There is no trial we cannot overcome with God by our side. He has equipped us with everything we need for success in life.

"Trials don't kill you. How you handle them is what makes or breaks you. I ran to God, and He restored my life and my heart. I'm not the stereotypical young, single mom that you hear about or watch on TV. I'm the young, single mom that strives after Jesus and is determined to share her story with others. I pray God uses my story to affect others, and I have no doubt that He will." –Olivia B.

Temptations can come at any time. I remember a time when I felt so close and connected with God, but even then, I was still tempted. I was at a place in my life where I felt so happy and fulfilled. I had two beautiful boys and a happy marriage. On an ordinary night, lying on my living room floor watching television, my thoughts took an ugly turn.

Go take some pills. It is time to end your life. No one needs you here anymore. They came from nowhere, but they seemed so real, so valid. I lay there on the floor, not wanting to move while these thoughts consumed my mind. Deep down I knew the truth. I knew that these thoughts were all lies and that Satan was trying to tempt me, but I still felt like I did not have the strength to get up. I just felt frozen. I knew I needed God to help me and to replace these lies with His thoughts for me. Over and over, I asked Him to help me. All of a sudden, a Gatorade commercial came on and caught my attention. It was as if the room went dark but a spotlight was on the TV. I zoned in, captured by the words and images I was watching. I saw an image of a man running down the sidewalk with drips of Gatorade streaming down his face like sweat. He kept running and running. Even though he looked exhausted, he wasn't going to give up. As I was watching this man running, the narrator said something that caused me to sit up instantly, "… when thoughts of suicide come, ignore the inner voices deep inside telling you to give up …"

I was blown away. God was speaking to me right in that moment through a television commercial! I started processing those words and realizing that I had power over the inner voices that were not my own and I did not have to listen to them. I knew I could stand up, stand firm and resist the devil and he must flee. God gave me the strength to stand up in that very moment. I walked over to my husband and climbed into his lap and he held me like a baby. I placed my head on his shoulder and rested in his arms. I was crying on the inside at first until the tears began to fall on the outside.

A few months later, I was at a freedom ministry class at Gateway church called Kairos. They asked us to close our eyes and ask God about a time when we felt alone and scared. I began to visualize the day I thought about taking my life. Then they said to ask God where He was when that event happened. So, with my eyes closed and remembering back to when I was lying on the floor and the flood of temptation came over me to end my life, I gently asked, "God, where were You? I want to see You in the room with me." It was then that He showed me that He embraced me as my husband held me. It was through my husband's arms He comforted me and a peace washed over me. He calmed all my fears and overwhelmed me with His love. He showed me that I was not alone and that He was with me the entire time. He will never let me go.

If you have experienced thoughts of suicide or thoughts of bringing harm upon yourself, I want to express with deep, heartfelt compassion that I am truly sorry you have felt those feelings. You are not alone. Do not be afraid to ask for help from your leaders. They want to help and can give you the resources to get through this. Cry out to God when you have moments you feel tempted. Ask Him to give you a sign like He did for me. He will use anything to speak to you and get your attention. You can look up to Him, and He will be your rescuer and defender. He will give you the strength to stand up, stand firm and live. Don't ever, ever, ever give up. Your life is so precious. You are loved and treasured. You are worth more than all the diamonds and rubies in the world. YOUR LIFE MATTERS. You have power over those thoughts. You are stronger than you think, and God is not finished with you; He is just getting started. Love life to the fullest and embrace it with no regrets. It is better to get your struggles out in the open and not keep secrets.

"I found out that not only did God love me, but I was HIS daughter and He was always there for me and always will be. All of the heavy burdens that I had been carrying on my shoulders had been lifted away when I forgave all those people who hurt me in my past. I gave it all to God, and when I did … I no longer felt the judgment. I no longer felt the neediness. I no longer hated myself." –Meaghan W.

"You are not alone if you have sacred secrets that shame you from participating in the great things God has planned for you … " –The Princess Within by Serita Ann Jakes. But it is time for you to confess to God the truth of your secret, so that He can free you from your past. There is no secret that can separate you from God's love. There is no secret that can separate you from His blessings. There is no secret worth keeping you from His grace.

This week, please take time to reflect and ask God to reveal any secrets that need to surface. He may bring back a memory, a thought, an impression or simply a word. If you feel comfortable, write it out and place it in a sealed envelope. If it is too personal and you do not feel comfortable writing it out, just pray and tell God that you no longer want to keep this secret from Him. He knows all that we have ever done or will do. He will not be shocked. He is ready for you to come out of hiding so He can share with you the plans He has for you. He is waiting and will listen … No more hiding, no more secrets, no more looking back!

We will step into the light and look forward to our days ahead with Jesus by our side.

God would surely have known it, for he knows the secrets of every heart. Psalm 44:21, emphasis mine

"Come now, let's settle this," says the Lord. "Though your sins are like scarlet, I will make them as white as snow. Though they are red like crimson, I will make them as white as wool." Isaiah 1:18

Carrying around secrets for a long time can be a heavy load. We carry them around like a heavy backpack that has been filled with so much stuff, extra baggage that we forgot we threw in months ago, and it is getting SO heavy! In this backpack, all those secrets we have kept may have resulted in some anger, impatience, bitterness, pride, hurt and so much more, that are stuffed down inside. We are ready to lighten the load!

One afternoon I passed by a little girl riding on her bicycle with her backpack over her shoulders. She was pedaling as fast as her little five-year-old legs could go, on her way to school. Her Dad was walking closely behind her. At one point she stopped pedaling and looked over at her Dad as if to say, *"This is way too much for me to carry. Can you take over for me?"* He held out his hands and took her backpack from her. He placed it on his shoulders. He took that heavy load from her. Would you like to remove your heavy backpack like she did and place it in God's hands? He can empty out all the unnecessary fillers that you placed inside. He can lighten your load.

Then Jesus said, "Come to me, all of you who are weary and carry heavy burdens, and I will give you rest. Take my yoke upon you. Let me teach you, because I am humble and gentle at heart, and you will find rest for your souls. For my yoke is easy to bear, and the burden I give you is light." Matthew 11:28-30

Prayer: *Holy Spirit, I ask that You would purify and heal my broken heart, that You would cleanse and renew my mind. With Your power, realign my will to Your will and prompt and convict me when I stray. Empower me to make healthy, godly choices. Please restore and refresh my emotions.*

Action:

What temptation have you faced in your past that you don't want to give in to again?

....
....
....
....
....
....
....
....
....
....

What trials have you been through that grew your faith and made you a stronger person?

....
....
....
....
....
....
....
....
....
....
....
....

Mommy's Heartbeat:

Who has been a great support to you during your pregnancy? How have they influenced your life?

....

....

....

....

....

....

....

....

....

....

....

....

....

....

....

....

....

....

....

....

....

....

....

Baby's Heartbeat:

Have you been nesting? In what ways at home have you been preparing your space for your baby?

....
....
....
....
....
....
....
....
....

Have you picked a color scheme or theme for the nursery? If you've chosen adoption, has the adoptive family made a place for the baby's arrival yet?

....
....
....
....
....
....
....
....
....
....
....
....

HEART CHECK:

What secrets are you ready to expose in exchange for grace and a lighter load?

Vindication

Embracing Forgiveness and Breaking the Chains

Vindication: to forgive, to clear from accusations, free from blame

Forgive: to grant pardon, release and stop blame

Justification: to excuse, apology

Vindication and forgiveness are a choice. The offended cannot do anything to take away the pain that has already started. Only God can take away the pain and mend a broken heart. God is waiting for you to come to Him. He wants you to bring all that pain and hurt to Him. All of those things belong on the cross anyway. You were never designed to carry all of the anguish that is a result of not forgiving someone. Forgiveness is the way you hand it over.

Ask yourself this question: *Who is it that owns a part of my brain at this time? Is there something or someone that is taking up residence and causing clutter? What do I keep rehearsing over and over again in my mind and cannot seem to let it go or resolve?* Usually the first person on the list holds the biggest part of it. They can become a stronghold and have a stranglehold upon the brain waves and stems in your mind until you can release it.

Forgiveness brings healing to our hearts and to others. Whenever we hold unforgiveness toward others and even ourselves in our hearts, it is like a virus or disease and begins to eat away at us. It can slowly or quickly cause damage to our hearts. This can also cause our hearts to become hardened as stone, and it takes more than a chisel to pick away at this "stuff." We may hold some hurts and wounds of things that happened to us as children. These things may be very hard to even think about, much less forgive.

"When we had class on forgiveness, God opened my heart about all the unforgiveness I had in my heart. I knew it was there, but He showed me how it was affecting my life. I forgave my dad for leaving us after I was born and never being there. I also forgave my mom for not being there for me when I needed her the most, during my pregnancy. Once I forgave her in my heart, something changed. She started being there for me, helping me and being a little more accepting of the baby boy I was carrying. I know God is going to restore our relationship even more." –Raven D.

There may be someone in your life that you are ready to forgive, but you need to set boundaries in place. Boundaries can be set in anger or love. When you form a judgment against someone who has offended you in a certain way, then your heart becomes hardened based on what someone else has done. They are able to walk around freely, but you are still carrying the offense. Maybe you are holding on to some anger or bitterness toward your parents for not attending your recitals or volleyball games, or not accepting and being supportive when you told them you were pregnant. When you allow *justification* to come in, to excuse and accept an apology, this will bring healing from the pain so that your heart can stop hurting. The only way to be free from all that "stuff" is forgiveness.

Your heart may also begin to build walls and resentment towards the person that did the offense. Some bitterness begins to grow over time, and before you know it, there is this giant ache of bitterness that is marked on your heart and you do not know how to get rid of it. You can try to put band aids on all these wounds and unforgiveness you have towards someone, but until your heart is fully healed, it will still eat at you and cause sleepless nights. The way to be fully healed is to release the hurt, let it go, choose to forgive, give them to God, and allow healing to take place.

Forgiveness isn't forgetting what happened to you. When you choose to forgive, you do not have to always trust that person, you are just freeing them from your thoughts and releasing them to God. When you look at an offense and say, "I can forgive him for _____, and then when he did this_____, and said _____, but I cannot ever forgive him for this _____." That isn't true forgiveness. You want to release it all.

When Jesus died on the cross, He paid the price for ALL of our sins. He doesn't look at some and say, "Oooh, that one is too bad, I cannot forgive her for that." No, He forgives us for everything—ALL sins that we have ever done, or sins that we will commit in our future. Just as He forgives all, WE must also forgive all.

Another definition of *justification* is "to declare innocent or guiltless." This is what Jesus gives to you freely. He declares you innocent. He sees you spotless and clean. He sees you free of guilt. Your sins are washed away because He paid the price on the cross.

As a child, I experienced a lot of mental and verbal abuse from my stepfather. I was so scared of him. He would throw things at me in anger and rage, and I walked around our home on egg shells not ever knowing what was going to set him off. I would jump when he entered the room, even if I wasn't doing anything wrong, because I was always startled by him.

God came in and touched that brokenness

One day, I got into HUGE trouble. I was to pull weeds outside and to pick up rocks and place them in piles. As I was pulling weeds in a flower bed, there were some bushes that looked to me as if they were dead. So I just decided to pull them out and toss them to the side for the compost pile. I thought I had done the right thing and was completely innocent in my thinking.

A little later, my stepfather came home and stormed in the house telling me to come outside. He asked me why on earth did I pull up the rose bushes? OOPS! I responded, "I did not know they were still alive, and I am so sorry I pulled them up by mistake." I received correction, and then was told to stay in the garage for several hours to think about my mistake. As an adult, I sometimes look back on the incident. I used to have a pain in my heart that cut deep. I chose to forgive my stepfather for all the things that he said and did to hurt my heart. A few years ago, I decided to write him a detailed letter forgiving him for the things he had said and done to me as a child. I needed to do this for closure. I mailed it to him as a final release. Making that choice to forgive and bring vindication to him helped to heal a place in my heart that was so raw and scarred.

God came in and touched that brokenness and heartache and brought healing and wholeness to my heart. He longs to do the same for you. Will you let Him? Maybe He might ask you to write a letter to that person. He might ask you to send them a message or call them. He knows your heart and He has the solution for the best way to respond in your situation. Just listen for His instruction; He is always there to guide you.

*"I still to this day remember the hardest part of **Embrace Grace** was actually saying, 'I forgive myself'—I am so thankful for all that I learned in **Embrace Grace**." –Brittany S.*

Just as we forgive others, we have to allow ourselves to be forgiven. We have to embrace God's forgiveness for all that we have done. Let go of the guilt, shame, regret, embarrassment, blame and burdens and give it all to God! He wants to take it ALL!

So just what IS the best way to forgive yourself? The answer is simple—give it all over to God. If you were to make a list of all of the things that you hold against yourself, you can easily see that you can be your worst enemy and critic. You may criticize yourself over past mistakes, follies and mix-ups and not even give yourself a chance. Allow yourself to be forgiven. Jesus already bore your shame and sins on the cross once and for all; it is a done deal. Allow the price that He paid for you to be complete in you. Receive His mercy and forgiveness for yourself. Forgiveness is a choice. Say it out loud as many times as you need to, "I CHOOSE TO FORGIVE MYSELF." Get used to saying it because you will always have times when you wish you had made a different choice. Just choose to forgive yourself and move forward.

Even if that person wrongs you seven times a day and each time turns again and asks forgiveness, you must forgive. Luke 17:4

Our hearts, like pink clay, can become hardened towards our parents, siblings, boyfriends or even God. These hurts may be recent or you may have carried them around for a really long time. You start to put up walls around your heart to prevent getting hurt or feeling the pain or stings again. It begins with a little brick, then another, because those words and actions really hurt, and before you know it, there is this huge wall that you cannot see over, crawl over or even get through. There is this space between you and this person, or God, which prevents you from really connecting—a space so big that seeing the truth, admitting that the offense may have been wrong on either party, and then releasing that person may seem impossible to do. With God's help and reading His Word, in time, the bricks and hardness will begin to crumble and soften. Walls are coming down! Sometimes it takes squeezing, pressing, rolling, holding and molding to soften the clay, and the same is true with your heart. Our prayer is that your heart will be softened and refined throughout this process. God is shaping, molding and refining you to become the mother that He desires you to be for your baby. The love and tenderness that comes when your hearts are softened is so precious. Ask God for guidance and to lead you through this softening and reformation. He is waiting to help you. Your heart will be your treasure.

"My once hard heart has now been softened." –Morgan B.

… O Lord, you are our Father. We are the clay, and you are the potter. We are all formed by your hand. Isaiah 64:8

But we have this treasure in earthen vessels, so that the surpassing greatness of the power will be of God, and not from ourselves. 2 Corinthians 4:7 NASB

Even with our scarlet letters, stains and sins, God says that if we come to Him and ask for forgiveness, He will take the ugly sins that we have in our life and wash them away. He covers us with His grace and makes us pure—white as snow. What a beautiful picture! Our sins are washed white as snow!

Have mercy on me, O God, because of your unfailing love. Because of your great compassion, blot out the stain of my sins. Wash me clean from my guilt. Purify me from my sin. For I recognize my rebellion … For I was born a sinner—yes, from the moment my mother conceived me. But you desire honesty from the womb, teaching me wisdom even there. Purify me from my sins and I will be clean; wash me, and I will be whiter than snow. Psalm 51:1-3, 5-7

… Though your sins are like scarlet, I will make them white as snow. Though they are red like crimson, I will make them as white as wool. Isaiah 1:18

Liberation and Emancipation—Liberty and freedom from the chains

Bondage can keep you locked up as if you were in prison or incarcerated. The cold jail cell and bars may not be visible to the naked eye, but you are trapped, nonetheless. You wonder, "How did it get this far? Where did I go wrong?" You may be carrying around a ball and chain around your ankles that you have no idea where it came from, or how to remove it. It is attached with chains, invisible chains that can only be removed by Jesus.

One of my best friends, Kerrie Oles, wrote a book titled, *Invisible Chains*. I encourage you to read her personal story and see for yourself how these chains can become a part of us. You can be so accustomed to them that they become a part of who you are … until you are made aware of them. You have a choice. You can walk around carrying the weight of the world, or you can choose to be set free from the bondage. Choose life, love and liberty and declare it!

The Spirit of the Lord God is upon me, because the Lord has anointed me to bring good news to the afflicted; He has sent me to bind up the brokenhearted, to proclaim liberty to captives and freedom to prisoners; to proclaim the favorable year of the Lord … Isaiah 61:1-2 NASB

Embrace your freedom!

He led them from the darkness and deepest gloom; he snapped their chains. Psalm 107:14

In that wonderful day when the Lord gives his people rest from sorrow and fear, from slavery and chains. Isaiah 14:3

But now, behold, I am freeing you today from the chains which are on your hands …
Jeremiah 40:4 NASB

"I have never been happier to get away from my past and break the chains that were holding me down. God has always been there for me and my son. He is a Father to the fatherless and provides over and above when the men in my life choose not to. And it doesn't matter that they don't because my God does and always will! Psalm 68:5-6 says 'A father to the fatherless, a defender of widows, is God in his holy dwelling. God sets the lonely in families …' And He reminds me daily that just because I had a baby at 20 years old, doesn't mean that I can't still fulfill the dreams He has placed in my heart." –Kaitlin W

"Blessings of Forgiveness Prayer" –source unknown

Prayer: *Father, I thank You that You have never rejected me and You never will. Even if other people reject me, You have received me unconditionally. I am accepted in Jesus. I thank You that my acceptance does not depend on anything but Jesus, His love, mercy, grace, sacrifice and righteousness. I am not ashamed before You. Thank You that I am completely forgiven and cleansed by the blood of Jesus. I will not allow the enemy to harass me about the past. I repent of my sins and choose to forgive myself and receive the full freedom of Your forgiveness. I thank You that my body can function in Your peace, fully healed and whole. My mind is at rest, and I choose to forget past failures and struggles and to enjoy Your love, Your thoughts and Your ways. What amazing grace that You remember my sins and iniquities no more! Jesus took them on Himself. Because of Jesus' forgiveness, I can forgive others in His name. As an act of my will, I choose to forgive all those who have hurt me, harmed me or spoken against me. I free them in my thoughts and no longer hold their sins against them. I ask You to bless them in Your mercy. I thank You that I am a brand new creation! All the old has passed away and I stand clean in Your sight. I choose to receive your healing grace by the cleansing power of the Holy Spirit within me. I'm thankful that You control me, not my emotions or what others say. I receive all Your blessings for my life and give You all praise, honor and glory. Amen!*

Action:

Is there something from your past that you need to apologize and ask for forgiveness for involving someone close to you, or even apologize to someone you may have formed a judgment against?

....

....

....

....

....

....

....

....

....

Who are you choosing to forgive so that you can free them from your thoughts and no longer hold their sins against them? Are you willing to finally forgive yourself for something that you have had a hard time letting go of?

....

....

....

....

....

....

....

....

....

Mommy's Heartbeat:

What has being pregnant taught you the most, so far? In what positive way has your baby changed your life? Is God softening your heart in certain areas of your life?

Baby's Heartbeat:

What good mommy advice have you received? If you are choosing adoption, what adoption advice have you received?

....
....
....
....
....
....
....
....
....
....
....

What has been your favorite part of being pregnant?

....
....
....
....
....
....
....
....
....
....
....

HEART CHECK:

What are the invisible chains that have made you feel anchored down for so long that you are ready to break free from through forgiveness and grace?

Transformation

Turning Away From Sin and Embracing Change

Transformation: complete change, change in form, nature or character, metamorphosis

Reflection: an image, thought or thinking, meditation, ponder, view

Repentance: reviewing one's actions and feeling contrition or sorrow

Allow yourself to see your reflection as God sees you and created you. His heart dances over you. He is acting on your behalf and rejoicing over you. He is FOR you. Let your heart dance with His. A happy heart brings elation, fullness of joy, and makes you want to shout from the rooftops. You will bring praise from your lips. When you share about His goodness, when you sing over your baby, when you share stories of love with others, your heart is singing a happy tune. Your heart is tuned to the heartbeat of Heaven. Rejoice with all your heart. Sing Him a new song.

… Look, I am making everything new … Revelation 21:5

Reading from the book of Psalms will always bring a song to your heart. These are penned from King David in Psalm 45. "*My heart is moved. My tongue is the pen of a skillful writer. Grace flows from your lips. Listen daughter, pay attention. There is a river- God is within her; she will not be toppled. God will help her when morning dawns.*"

"*After attending* **Embrace Grace**, *I started seeing a transformation in myself. A seed was being planted in my soul by these selfless, wonderful, amazing women that I spent time with every week. I started to think differently about my circumstances and I began to see the great joy and miracle my baby was to me. My baby saved my life. My son put my life back on track and into perspective. I had no idea how amazing being a mother was going to be while I was pregnant—I could only imagine; but it was even more than I could have dreamed when I finally laid eyes on my blessing.*" –Stephanie S.

One of my favorite songs is Kari Jobe's song, "You are Good." Read these words … "*Your kindness leads me to repentance, Your goodness draws me to Your side. Your mercy calls me to be like You, and Your favor is my delight. You are good and Your mercy is forever.*" I love the simplicity of this song. God saw that everything He made, His whole creation, was good. God is complete goodness. He cannot be bad. We said a prayer as littler girls that said, "*God is good, God is great, let us thank Him for our food. Amen.*" It's so simple and easy. He wants it to be just as easy to repent of our sins, humble ourselves and turn to Him. He wants us to seek His face and not look back toward the world. He wants to transform our hearts so that our desires match up to His. His perfect will and love is where we find our ultimate happiness and peace. His goodness leads us to turn away from our sins.

… God's kindness is intended to lead you to repentance. Romans 2:4

Repentance not only says, "I'm sorry," but also says, "I don't want to do that again and I am going to turn away from my sin." True repentance is when we decide to go in a different direction. It's for us to *change*. God is pleased when we change our minds and hearts and repent from our sinful ways. Having a repentant heart is like a gift to God. He will take that gift and lead you to change. He doesn't drag you to repentance, He points the way. He gently leads, but you have to look to Him as you have a change of heart. When we see God's grace and goodness, our hearts change from wanting the things of this world to wanting Him, His love and glory! The more we pursue after Him in love, the bigger victory we have over our sins. Pursuing God transforms our hearts and lives!

If you could have a remote control and somehow rewind back to the moment you found out that you were pregnant, remember some of the emotions you felt. That moment was probably a roller coaster of emotions. All of the opinions and observations of others may have caused you to walk with your head held down and to feel ashamed or want to run and hide. Now hit the fast forward button a little bit … ok, now pause. You somehow opened this book, *Embraced by Grace.* Maybe you are taking an **Embrace Grace** class, maybe you heard about it from a friend … the possibilities are numerous as to how this book is in your hands at this moment; however, it is not a coincidence or a random act in any way. You were meant to go through this journey for a reason. As you have been reading through and engaging your heart into all that God has for you, your heart has been changing a little bit at a time. It was not an instant or drastic change, it was a progressive change—a type of transformation.

Now I would like you to use your imagination. Try to visualize in your mind as you read this transformation.

In the beginning stage there is an egg. A very tiny egg. This egg is given nutrients and begins to grow. A small change begins to emerge, but almost invisible to the naked eye. A hatching of some sort occurs. A caterpillar then begins emerging from the egg. This caterpillar is very hungry. It begins to chew and munch and eat everything in sight. It eats all the luscious green leaves it can find. It is storing up for a time of suspense. It begins to feel something different is about to happen, but is unsure of what that "something" is. It is content for the time being to just crawl around and continue eating. Soon the caterpillar is inching its way on a branch or a tree, and that time of suspense arrives.

A cocoon begins to cover the caterpillar, and it is hung there in a suspended state for a period of time. While inside the cocoon, amazing things are happening, but this little caterpillar hasn't the slightest idea of what is about to happen. While in the utter seclusion of being inside the cocoon, the Creator is up to some impressive artwork. He begins to paint a masterpiece. He is busily at work, all the while the caterpillar has no idea what is being done. God only knows exactly what happens inside of there. Maybe she is asleep for a short period of time, as in a hibernation stage. She may begin to think, "how long is this going to take? I feel I am ready now. But how much longer? I must be ready now." No, not quite yet. Just a touch here, and a little more there. Almost, it's almost time.

"Turn over your sense of impatience to Me," the Creator says. "Let Me refine you completely during this process." She begins to turn over and trade in all her sense of desires and selfish ambitions to her Creator. He is making a spectacle out of her. He is a wonderful Maker. He whispers, "Ok, now it's time." He blows with His mighty breath and the cocoon disappears. From the emersion of the cocoon comes forth a beautiful butterfly… a painted lady spreads her wings and begins to fly. She flutters her wings. The breeze whips around her. She feels lovely. She feels pretty. She feels secure. She knows that a transformation has just taken place.

You can get comfortable in your safe environment; but look out into the world-know there is so much more for you to see.

You are that painted lady. You are the butterfly that has gone through a transformation. You have encountered many stages along the way. In your cocoon stage, you were chewing and munching on the nuggets of scriptures and lessons along the way. You were hungry to know more and unsure of what was about to happen. During this time of suspension being trapped up in the cocoon, you were not sure if you liked being stuck inside this tight space. It felt uncomfortable. You maybe wanted to rush the process. You may have sometimes even said, "Just fix me already!" But your Maker knows you and knitted you so uniquely, and He knows that His timing is best. He has been painting and mending and repairing all of you during your stages, and now look how beautiful your wings are! The flapping of your wings really does matter. Time to spread your wings and fly into motherhood and everything that God has destined you to be!

The flapping of your wings, the movements, actions and reactions that you make have an impact on not only your life, but your baby's life, and the countless lives of millions around you for generations to come. Your life truly does matter. Your life has a destiny and purpose for greatness. You will help to change the world by one heartbeat, two heartbeats, three and then four heartbeats multiplying over and over. If we all have the connected heartbeat of Heaven, in unity and together, we will achieve great things lined up with our Father's heartbeat.

On our first night of our third semester of *Embrace Grace*, I brought a little clear solo cup that had some tiny eggs inside on little green leaves. I brought them to class each week so the girls could see the different stages of the butterfly. Each week, there was a small progression in the stages. The caterpillar stage, then the cocoon, and then the painted lady emerged. We were all mesmerized by the miracle of this process. The time came for us to release the butterflies. They were in a green butterfly habitat and were very content inside. When we lifted the lid to release them, the butterflies did not fly away at first. They were very happy inside in their comfortable surroundings. However, when we nudged them and they realized they could flap their beautiful wings and actually fly away, they were off in a moment's time and were free—never looking back.

The same can be true for you. Maybe you have been content in your surroundings and not sure about spreading your wings to fly. You can get comfortable in your safe environment; but look out into the world—know there is so much more for you to see. It's time! Your transformation has come and you too can be a part of the movement. You no longer have to be held back, but you can be the girl that God has destined you to be. You have so much beauty on the inside of you. Are you ready to see all that He has created you to be? This is what this transformation has been all about. Everything you have been through so far in your life has made you into the beautiful person you are today. He lovingly rearranges your heart from the inside out. He makes all things beautiful. This is your new beginning. It is a new season. Beauty is seen when He looks at you. He doesn't want you to hide behind a mask, He made you lovely. He wants to see you.

"God took my ugly and destructive life; He used my unplanned pregnancy to give me a new life, a fresh start, a purpose, and the greatest joy I know … It seems like it was all done as a gift to me; but really it is all for His glory. My God certainly works in mysterious ways. For this, I am humbly grateful."—Amber S.

From the time we are little girls and begin to start growing up, we start comparing ourselves to others and develop misconceptions. We put on a mask and start to hide behind it so that people cannot see who we really are inside. We are afraid of what they might really see. We put on a happy face and smile and pretend that everything is fine. We feel the need to fit in and to look cool. We feel the need to be accepted. Everyone has so many expectations of what we should be and who we should become, starting at first with our parents, then teachers and coaches at school. Friends and classmates give their opinions of what they think we should do, who we should be, what we should wear, what size we should be and where we should go. Then we start dating, and our boyfriends tell us how we should act, feel and look. The world has so many unrealistic expectations of the way we should look when God made us perfect. We cover up our own emotions, suppress them and push really far down inside. So many feelings that we want to feel, but do not know how to because we have been hiding behind this mask for so long. Stop and think. *Who do you really want to be?*

Close your eyes and picture yourself just being you. No pretending, no acting, no hidden agendas or fears. Just YOU! You are a beautiful, amazing, remarkable and talented YOU. Let's take off the masks and reveal who is truly behind the mask. No more hiding. No more fears and tears. No more worries. No more regrets.

But we all, with unveiled face, beholding as in a mirror the glory of the Lord, are being transformed into the same image from glory to glory, just as by the Spirit of the Lord.
2 Corinthians 3:18 NKJV

Remember the movie Bambi? The sweet little deer Bambi and a little doe meet by the water's edge to take a drink. They looked down at the water and see the reflections of themselves. They take a really long look at each other and she gives him some pointers about life and who he really is. She also begins to tell him what is expected of him as a prince in the forest. Have you ever looked at yourself in a body of water to see the reflection of your face?

As a face is reflected in water, so the heart reflects the real person. Proverbs 27:19

Allow yourself to see your reflection as God sees you and created you. Look in the mirror and gaze deeply into your eyes. Wait there for a moment. Soak it all in. You are a Princess. You are God's little girl, and He adores you and created you with a perfect reflection. He does not see any flaws or imperfections. What once was broken, is now made whole. He sees grace and beauty. You are His chosen one. He delights in you. He will fill your heart full of love.

When I was a child, I spoke and thought and reasoned as a child. But when I grew up, I put away childish things. Now we see things imperfectly as in a cloudy mirror, but then we will see everything with perfect clarity. All that I know now is partial and incomplete, but then I will know everything completely, just as God now knows me completely. Three things will last forever—faith, hope, and love—and the greatest of these is love. 1 Corinthians 13:11-13

And so, God willing, we will move forward to further understanding. For it is impossible to bring back to repentance those who were once enlightened— those who have experienced the good things of heaven and shared in the Holy Spirit, who have tasted the goodness of the word of God and the power of the age to come. Hebrews 6:3-5

Arise, shine; for your light has come! And the glory of the Lord is risen upon you. For behold, the darkness shall cover the earth, and deep darkness the people; but the Lord will arise over you, and His glory will be seen upon you. Isaiah 60:1 NKJV

Prayer: *"God, please forgive me for my sins. I repent and turn away from that sin and turn to you. Fill me up with your kindness and love. Show me a reflection of how you see me—pure and holy. Give me strength to not ever go back to that sin. It has no hold on me because I cling tightly to You, my heavenly Father."*

Action:

What transformations have you already seen happening in your life since you started *Embraced by Grace*?

....
....
....
....
....
....
....
....
....
....

What qualities, physically and within your personality, do you like about yourself? What traits have you tried to hide that you now would like to show and embrace the person God created you to be?

....
....
....
....
....
....
....
....
....
....

Mommy's Heartbeat:

What scripture(s) has (have) encouraged you most during your pregnancy? What does it (do they) mean to you?

....

....

....

....

....

....

....

....

....

....

....

....

....

....

....

....

....

....

....

....

....

....

....

Baby's Heartbeat:

What do you wish most for your baby?

....
....
....
....
....
....
....
....
....
....
....

Have you had any vivid pregnancy dreams?

....
....
....
....
....
....
....
....
....
....
....

HEART CHECK:

What sins are you ready to turn away from so that you can experience the beautiful transformation that God has for you?

Grace

Just Grace

"I'm lying here holding my baby girl and I just got this moment of overwhelming peace and I thought to myself 'I wish I could just freeze this moment, because there is no way it can ever be any better than this.' Then I felt His presence as He told me that He has BIG plans in store for me and to hold on tight." –Devin S.

Grace: The elegance or beauty of form, favor or good will, mercy or pardon, the freely given and unmerited favor of God.

Grace is a gift, a free gift. And all we have to do is simply receive it. It is not a gift you or I can earn, nor is it a gift we deserve, but it is ours for the taking, and it is a priceless, beautiful gift. When we grasp the true meaning of grace and see for ourselves the treasure and pleasure that it brings, we are never the same. We walk with a spring in our step, a smile on our face, a fresh outlook on life—all because we have been touched by the gift of grace. We will know without a doubt God loves us and covers us. No matter what, He is always here to hold us, to embrace us, to love our hearts.

"Grace is God intervening. Grace forgives us for our sins, big and small and everything in between. Grace is freely given. Freely received. Grace is unconditional. Grace accepts us for who we are. Grace provides for a greater future. We can experience grace, reflect grace and extend grace. Little choices today predetermine our destiny. Be ready to shine for Jesus lavishly!" –Pastor Debbie Morris

So we praise God for the glorious grace he has poured out on us who belong to his dear Son. He is so rich in kindness and grace that he purchased our freedom with the blood of his Son and forgave our sins. He has showered his kindness on us, along with all wisdom and understanding. Ephesians 1:6-8

Let's face it … things do not always go right. Moments in time or even entire months can feel out of control and not the way you planned for them to go. You have to give yourself grace. As much as we plan and schedule and prepare, there is always a chance for some hiccups along the way.

One afternoon as I finished nursing and burping my three month-old baby, we were cuddling peacefully when I noticed he had four tiny purple dots in the shape of an arrow pointing upward on the back of his little head. I quickly grabbed my giant book full of all kinds of information about babies. After searching for these symptoms, I slammed the book shut, refusing to receive what I discovered in the book. The diagnosis this book gave, based on the symptoms I looked up, was very life-threatening. I began to pray over my son and called some very close friends, asking them to pray, as well. I also made an appointment with his pediatrician for that afternoon. I had to wait two hours before heading to their office, and in those two hours I held him so closely, and I felt my faith begin to grow stronger. Listening to worship music, I heard these encouraging lyrics pouring from the speakers:

"I will lift my eyes to the Maker of the mountains I can't climb. I will lift my eyes to the Calmer of the oceans raging wild. I will lift my eyes to the Healer of the hurt I hold inside. I will lift my eyes to You." –Lift My Eyes by Bebo Norman

These lyrics are based on Psalm 121:1, and my heart filled with hope to not worry and become consumed with fear. I began to focus my attention on God and not the possibilities of some health issue for my baby, looking to God as his healer. I began to focus on miracles.

Driving to his pediatrician that afternoon, I had a few tears streaming down my cheeks. But it was not because of fear. It was because I felt God so near, as if He was holding me and whispering to me, "*It's going to be ok. Do not worry. Trust in me.*" My son's pediatrician gave him a checkup and a clear diagnosis without any alarm. He said some blood vessels had just busted from coughing so much. My son would need some breathing treatments, but other than that he was perfectly fine. What a sigh of relief! I had a choice to fear or to trust. I chose to trust in Jesus. God's grace overwhelmed me in this moment—it had covered my worries and given me the power to withstand the doctor appointment with my son, no matter the concern I had for him. God was embracing us both during a scary time.

No matter what you may be experiencing—maybe a health issue of your own like a high-risk pregnancy, or reports of concern for your baby—I want to express my deepest and most sincere heart cry and say that I am so sorry for any of these that you may encounter. God is holding your heart and will bring you comfort. You have a choice to fear the possibilities and "what if" scenarios or to trust God and know that He has the outcome safely in His hands. His grace covers you. His grace is the free gift mentioned above. The one where nothing you could do or say could earn this gift He longs to freely cover you with, to protect you and encourage you through every moment.

… and by His stripes we are healed! Isaiah 53:5 NKJV

… I have heard your prayer and seen your tears, I will heal you … 2 Kings 20:5

He forgives all my sins and heals all my diseases. Psalm 103:3

Songs can capture my attention probably more than anything. Songs and worship hold a sweet spot in my heart. A song by Hillsong United titled, *Rhythms of Grace* always speaks so tenderly to my heart. For a long time, I had the words mixed up and would sing "I am caught in the *ribbons* of grace." I visualized long strands of ribbon tied up from the sky, with many people entangled in these ribbons full of grace. The ribbons would graze our faces as we ran through a meadow full of flowers. Ribbons of all different colors and textures, rainbow colors, pinks and purples, blues and yellows, green polka dot—I pictured TONS of ribbons. Then to my surprise when I was typing out the lyrics to the song one day, I noticed that the words were not ribbons of grace, but rhythms of grace. "I am caught in the *rhythms* of grace." I laughed at myself and thought how silly I was.

But both my made-up lyrics and the actual lyrics perfectly portray grace. Ribbons and rhythms. Ribbons are tied to make bows. Bows are given on gifts. You are a precious gift. Your baby is a precious gift. There may be days when you feel as if your ribbons are tattered and you are barely hanging on. Just hold tight. Grace will meet you there. Rhythms of grace. Your life is a rhythm. As you sway to the music, baby in your womb, or in your arms, you are caught up in the rhythms of grace. You can feel God's heartbeat, His rhythm. His heartbeat beats along with your heartbeat for you and your baby. No matter what you have encountered, chosen, or done in your past or feel defeated from right now, you are still worthy of His grace and love. His grace is what captured you, entangling you like beautiful ribbons would, swooping you into His arms and leading you to your destiny and the good plans He has for you. His grace will give you the power to accomplish whatever lies before you each day. God longs to love you and provide for you in ways far above and beyond what you might think.

God can do anything you know—far more than you could ever imagine or guess or request in your wildest dreams… Ephesians 3:20 The Message

Toward the end of each semester we throw **Embrace Grace** ladies a baby shower. People from church and all around the community sign up to bring gifts for each mommy. There is nothing required from each mommy, but to show up and receive the gift with graciousness and gratitude. The **Embrace Grace** mommies and family and friends at the showers are always blown away with how each need has been covered above and beyond the way they imagined. Down to the details of the theme for the baby's nursery, or the mommy's favorite color, gifts are lavished on the girls and their babies. This is just a glimpse of the way God wants to pour out blessings and favor on your life simply because He loves you. No sin, attitude, or bad decision could disqualify you from this love. Not a single bad day could keep His grace from encompassing your life and helping you move forward with all that you need.

We have story after story of God's Operation Blessings at work in our lives for you and your little ones. Once we received a call from Food for the Soul, who donated 170 boxes of cereal to us. And Food for the Soul also connected us with Open Door Ministry, who blessed us with five pallets of diapers, wipes, feminine products, toilet paper and more! He has called you to be a part of *Embrace Grace* to show you these blessings, this love, these provisions, just to love on you, to tell you He is for you and not against you! He wants to be your Provider, your Healer, your Friend, your Love, whatever you need.

… I will open the windows of heaven for you. I will pour out a blessing so great you won't have enough room to take it in! Try it! Put me to the test! Malachi 3:10

After our very first *Embrace Grace* semester, we passed out a single diaper with a cute little ribbon and note attached to it reading: "You are changing the world one little diaper at a time." The diaper-changing can sometimes seem like it is never ending, but God sees every little diaper that you change, every little bottom that you wipe, every little face that you wash, and He says, "Thank you, My daughter for caring, loving and nurturing your children I have blessed you with."

"The most amazing thing just happened at Target! We were buying my baby stocking stuffers and were using the last money we had, and while we were waiting in line, the sweetest lady in front of us whispered something in the clerk's ear. All of a sudden she scans our stuff! We look at the clerk with confusion and the lady looks back at us, smiles and says, 'Merry Christmas!' The lady bought all of ours toys for us! It brought tears to my eyes … People are so amazing and God is so great!" –Kyndal O.

And he said to me, "My grace is sufficient for you, for My strength is made perfect in weakness." Therefore most gladly I will rather boast in my infirmities, that the power of Christ may rest upon me." 2 Corinthians 12:9 NKJV

For the Lord our God is our sun and our shield. He gives us grace and glory. The Lord will withhold no good thing from those who do what is right. Psalm 84:11

He is so rich in kindness and grace that he purchased our freedom with the blood of his Son and forgave our sins. Ephesians 1:7

So let us come boldly to the throne of our gracious God. There we will receive his mercy, and we will find grace to help us when we need it most. Hebrews 4:16

At the end of it all, our desire is to be held in God's arms. We long to be embraced by God's grace, to feel His loving arms surround us and hold us tightly and know He will never let us go—that no matter where this life takes us, no matter what surprises come our way, we can be found in God's embrace. He loves to comfort you.

As one whom his mother comforts, so I will comfort you … Isaiah 66:13

Celebration—The finish line within sight

Now is a time to celebrate life—you are pregnant and so close to bringing life into this world! We pray you and your precious baby live a blessed life your whole lives long!

May your coins be multiplied for you and your purse never empty. We pray that God's provision, protection and blessings pour out and overflow onto you and your family.

We pray your faith is always trusting in God to provide when things seem impossible.

He makes ALL things possible in His timing. Those who wait upon the Lord will renew their strength.

And may The Strong God—may He give you His blessings, blessings tumbling out of the skies, blessings bursting up from the Earth— blessings of breasts and womb. Genesis 49:25 The Message

Prayer: *Father, today I choose to receive your grace. I ask for your help to walk in grace daily, embracing it for myself and my baby and also extending it to others. I choose to trust you, giving you every fear, worry and tear. Thank you that I no longer have to walk in my own strength, trying to figure things out in my own abilities. Thank you that your grace covers every step I take and decision I make. Amen!*

Action:

In what areas of your life are you finally ready to accept God's grace?

....
....
....
....
....
....
....
....
....
....

How do you see God differently than you have before?

....
....
....
....
....
....
....
....
....
....

Mommy's Heartbeat:

Looking back over your pregnancy, what evidence have you seen that God has loved and protected you and your baby?

....

....

....

....

....

....

....

....

....

....

....

....

....

....

....

....

....

....

....

....

....

....

....

....

Baby's Heartbeat:

What was your favorite part of the *Embrace Grace* baby shower? If you are choosing adoption, have you set a date for your celebration of life shower?

....
....
....
....
....
....
....
....
....
....
....

Do you feel a bond or connection with your baby as he or she is growing in your womb or growing in your arms?

....
....
....
....
....
....
....
....
....
....
....

HEART CHECK:

Can you see how much God really and truly loves you? Has God changed your heart? Who does God say you are?

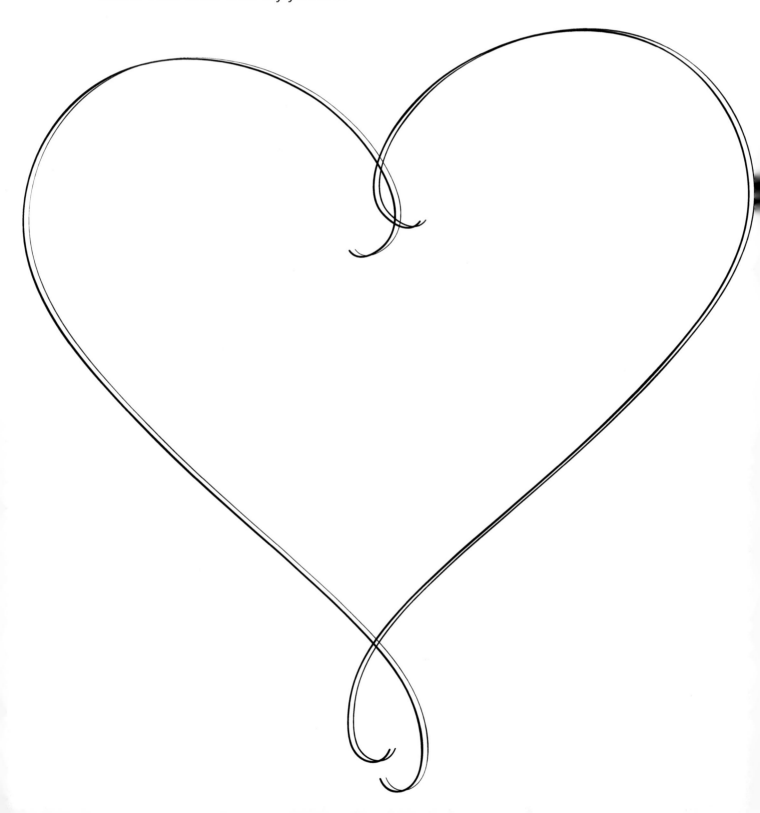

Conclusion

Where One Journey Ends, Another Begins

By now you might be very close to having your sweet baby. You have probably made the choice to either bless another family with your baby or keep your baby, and you feel at peace about your decision. You may already be holding your baby in your arms and your season of being a new mommy has begun!

Life is changing quickly, and you have done so well with trusting in God and holding His hand tightly as you walk through this new adventure together. There may have been times you felt like you could not make it another day ... but you did. There may be times in your future when you think you never predicted being young and with a baby, but now you cannot imagine your life without him or her. Sometimes you felt the weight of the world on your shoulders, but now you are lighter after giving those burdens to God and trusting Him fully. Some of the greatest revelations from God come during the times we feel the most broken.

Do you feel stronger? Because you are! With God, ALL things are possible! Don't ever forget the miracles God did for you during this season. Take the time to journal and write each of those miracles down so they are forever sealed in your heart. One thing in life is certain: there will be trials and bumps. There are always doors closing and new ones opening. We will face hurdles to jump over and hoops to jump through, but we can always be expectant about our future. We can learn to deal with one moment at a time, but not overshadow the dreams we have for our future. Whether handling unfinished business, paying off debt, getting another job, or meeting your husband, the distractions are endless. If we wait until life and all of its circumstances are just perfect, our dreams will never ever come true.

A new life and a big change in your life start with you.

Whatever the date is today, think about this exact date next year. Do you want to have moved forward, accomplished a goal (or several), and made steps toward your dream? Then you have to start TODAY. Even if it feels like the tiniest baby step, if you take one little step every day for a year, you will have accomplished a giant leap toward your destiny.

Achieving your dreams might mean you need to leave some people behind that are holding you back. If you are still holding on to a guy whom you hope will change someday, but at the moment, does nothing to support, encourage and motivate you, it might be time to let him go. Does he hold you back … or does he inspire you? Maybe you have a friend who is always making unwise choices and getting into trouble, and every time you are with him or her you find yourself in a situation you are uncomfortable with. It might be time to let that person go. Please pray about the people God wants in your life and whom He wants you to distance from.

Often after having your baby, all the friends that drifted away during the pregnancy start creeping back in again. And it is easy to fall back into the patterns you were in before you were pregnant. It is good to set boundaries and create guidelines for yourself NOW, before the temptations arise … because you WILL be tempted. Life is much easier when we resist temptation because we have already set boundaries for ourselves regarding bad influences. There will be times when we regretfully make decisions, and we just have to get back up, brush ourselves off and move forward again. Every day is a fresh start and a new beginning.

The closer and more intimate relationship you have with God, the easier it is to make good decisions that you can be proud of. You do not have to concentrate so much on what you can or cannot do, but focus on God—He will align your heart with His.

With God's help, you can make changes now that will be steps toward your dreams. If you are stuck with an awful job, He can line up the perfect job or schooling opportunity, just seek Him. If you are in a relationship where someone is treating you horribly and you put up with it for fear of being alone, just seek Him. He will give you the strength to close that door! His thoughts are higher than your thoughts. His plans are WAY bigger than what you could ever think or dream! He is a big God and He is FOR you! He opens doors that no man can slam shut. He is orchestrating all the connections for your dreams to be fulfilled. He is strategically placing new people in your life that will help you stay on God's path and in His perfect will. He will use all of these bumpy and difficult seasons you experienced to launch you into your destiny!

He will pour out blessings from His heart to yours

You are held safely in His arms. You and your baby are embraced by grace every moment of your lives. He will never leave you nor forsake you. You are His child forever. You belong to Him, and He longs to embrace you all the days of your life. He will pour out blessings from His heart to yours. Reach out your arms and embrace Him as you walk through the days, months, and seasons of your journey.

May the God of your father help you; may the Almighty bless you with the blessings above, and blessings of the watery depths below, and blessings of the breasts and womb. Genesis 49:25

** We are always looking for and are excited to receive testimonials from *Embrace Grace*. Did God do a work in your heart? Did you learn something new? Did a miracle happen in your life? Did God do a complete transformation in your heart? We want to hear about it! Go to www.iEmbraceGrace.com and tell us about it!

Prayers for Baby

Prayer is powerful! Pray over your baby in your womb every chance you get. Feel free to add your own prayers to add to this section and share with your *Embrace Grace* classmates!

SALVATION:

Lord, draw sweet [baby] to You at a very young age. Give him/her a heart for You and integrated in Your Word and Your Kingdom work. Let [baby] have a heart for worship and a passion for his/her relationship with You.

Drip down, O heavens, from above, and let the clouds pour down righteousness; let the earth open up and salvation bear fruit, and righteousness spring up with it. I, the Lord, have created it. Isaiah 45:8 NASB

So I am willing to endure anything if it will bring salvation and eternal glory in Christ Jesus to those God has chosen. 2 Timothy 2:10

GROWTH IN GRACE:

Lord, let [baby] grow in grace and in the knowledge of You. Let him/her be an example to others of how to walk in grace and how to constantly grow in his/her personal relationship with You.

The Child continued to grow and become strong, increasing in wisdom; and the grace of God was upon Him. Luke 2:40 NASB

Rather, you must grow in the grace and knowledge of our Lord and Savior Jesus Christ. All glory to him, both now and forever. Amen. 2 Peter 3:18

LOVE:

Lord, give [baby] a heart full of love for You, his/her family, his/her friends, and Your Word. Help him/her to shine brightly for You by showing Your love to all those with whom he/she has contact in life. Give him/her an understanding of Your love for him/her so that he/she may, in the same way, love others.

And walk in love, just as Christ also loved you and gave Himself up for us, an offering and a sacrifice to God as a fragrant aroma. Ephesians 5:2 NASB

Little children, let us not love with word or tongue, but in deed and trust. 1 John 3:18 NASB

HONESTY AND INTEGRITY:

Jesus, may honesty and integrity be [baby]'s virtues and his/her protection. May he/she walk in truth and never be afraid to admit his/her mistakes so that his/her integrity will be known. May he/she always be above reproach in his/her thoughts and actions.

May integrity and honesty protect me, for I put my hope in you. Psalm 25:21

Declare me innocent, O Lord, for I have acted with integrity; I have trusted in the Lord without wavering. Psalm 26:1

SELF-CONTROL:

Lord, please help [baby] to be set apart from others around him/her by being under your control. Teach him/her to not rely on instant gratification, but to develop patience so that he/she may have self-control.

So be on your guard, not asleep like the others. Stay alert and be clearheaded.
1 Thessalonians 5:6

PERSERVERANCE:

God, please teach [baby] to persevere in all he/she does, and help him/her to "*... run with endurance the race God has set before us*" (Hebrews 12:1). Help him/her not to give up easily, but to finish everything his/her hands start.

LOVE FOR GOD'S WORD:

Lord, may [baby] grow to find Your Word "*... more desirable than gold, yes, than much fine gold; sweeter also than honey and the drippings of the honeycomb*" (Psalm 19:10 NASB). Let Your Word come alive to him/her and let him/her live what he/she reads and believes.

HUMILITY:

God, cultivate in sweet [baby]'s heart the ability to "*... show true humility toward all*" (Titus 3:2). Help him/her to be quick to admit his/her mistakes and sins to his/her parents and to You. Help him/her not struggle with pride, but always be humble.

JUSTICE:

God, help [baby] to love justice as You do and to act justly in all he/she does.

He has told you, O man, what is good; and what does the Lord require of you but to do justice, to love kindness and to walk humbly with your God. Micah 6:8 NASB

For the righteous Lord loves justice. The virtuous will see his face. Psalm 11:7

MERCY:

Lord, help [baby] be merciful as You, his/her Father, is merciful (see Luke 6:36). Help him/her not to be hard on others, but to show them love, patience and mercy. Give him/her the ability to look at others the way You do and to have the mind of Christ toward them.

COMPASSION:

Lord, clothe [baby] with the virtue of compassion. Help him/her to be kind and loving to others and to be sensitive to others' needs before his/her own.

So as those who have been chosen of God, holy and beloved, put on a heart of compassion, kindness, humility, gentleness and patience. Colossians 3:12 NASB

RESPECT: (for self, others and authority)

Lord, please help [baby] to show respect to everyone and to come under the authority of those You place him/her under. Help him/her to be an obedient child, submissive to Your Word. Help him/her to "*respect everyone, and love your Christian brothers and sisters. Fear God, and respect the king.*" (1 Peter 2:17).

RESPONSIBILITY:

Lord, help [baby] to be responsible, one whom others can depend on. Help his/her word to mean something—help him/her to always follow through on all commitments he/she makes, not just the easy ones to fulfill. Help him/her to "*… bear his own load*" (Galatians 6:5 NASB).

STRONG, BIBLICAL SELF-ESTEEM:

God, please help [baby] to develop a strong self-esteem that is rooted in the realization that he/she is, "*… His (God's) workmanship, created in Christ Jesus…*" (Ephesians 2:10), and that he/she is fearfully and wonderfully made. Give him/her confidence, not in himself/herself, but in You through him/her.

CONTENTMENT:

God, give [baby] complete contentment in who he/she is, whose he/she is, and in all situations and circumstances he/she faces in his/her life.

I know how to live on almost nothing or with everything. I have learned the secret of living in every situation, whether it is with a full stomach or empty, with plenty or little. For I can do everything through Christ, who gives me strength. Philippians 4:12-13

FAITHFULNESS:

Lord, let [baby] have love and faithfulness. Help these things to never leave him/her. "*Never let loyalty and kindness leave you! Tie them around your neck as a reminder. Write them deep within your heart*" (Proverbs 3:3).

SELF DISCIPLINE:

Lord, I pray that [baby] develops self-discipline, I pray that he/she may "*… live disciplined and successful lives, to help them do what is right, just, and fair*" (Proverbs 1:3).

COURAGE:

Lord, please give [baby] boldness and courage in You. Help him/her to never be paralyzed by fear, for we know that fear is of the enemy. Help him/her to stand firm in You, even when those around him/her waver. Help him/her to be brave because he/she knows You are his/her Rock.

This is my command—be strong and courageous! Do not be afraid or discouraged. For the Lord your God is with you wherever you go. Joshua 1:9

HOPE:

God, let Your hope fill [baby] to overflowing with hope. Help him/her to know there is hope in all things because You are with him/her, providing everlasting hope.

I pray that God, the source of hope, will fill you completely with joy and peace because you trust in him. Then you will overflow with confident hope through the power of the Holy Spirit. Romans 15:13

PURITY:

Lord, create in [baby] a pure heart, and let others know him/her for purity. Give him/her the ability to think only on pure things, things of You, and to combat the enemy when he tries to have him/her distracted by impure, ungodly thoughts.

The precepts of the Lord are right, rejoicing the heart; the commandment of the Lord is pure, enlightening the eyes. Psalm 19:8 NASB

KINDNESS:

Lord, help [baby] to always be kind to other people. Let his/her heart, first thought, tendency and instincts be those of kindness. Give him/her the ability to draw people in with his/her kind heart so that he/she may show them Your love for them.

Instead, be kind to each other, tenderhearted, forgiving one another, just as God through Christ has forgiven you. Ephesians 4:32

WILLINGNESS TO WORK HARD:

God, please teach [baby] to value work and to work hard at everything he/she does, "... *working for the Lord rather than for people*" (Colossians 3:23). Whatever he/she does in life, Lord, let him/her do it with all his/her heart.

GENEROSITY:

Lord, help [baby] to be generous, always willing to share all that You give him/her. Help him/her to understand, at a young age, that every good gift comes from You and that he/she is merely a manager of those gifts.

Let them do good, that they may be rich in good works, ready to give, willing to share, storing up for themselves a good foundation for the time to come, that they may lay hold on eternal life. 1 Timothy 6:18-19 NKJV

PEACE:

Let [baby] love peace, Lord. Help him/her to be a peacemaker, one who does not "stir others up," but who helps them walk in peace. Give him/her a legacy of peace in his/her life. Guard him/her from fighting jealousy and rage and fill him/her with peace that passes understanding.

Therefore, let us pursue the things which make for peace and the things by which one may edify another. Romans 14:19 NKJV

JOY:

Help [baby] understand that Your joy is his/her strength, Lord.

You also became imitators of us and of the Lord, having received the word in much tribulation with the joy of the Holy Spirit. 1 Thessalonians 1:6 NASB

FAITH:

Lord, let faith find root in [baby]'s heart and grow there for all his/her years; that by faith he/she may gain what has been promised to him/her (see Luke 17:5-6). Help him/her to be protected from doubts and confusion and to have strong faith in You and Your Word.

SERVANT HEART:

Lord, give precious [baby] a servant's heart so that he/she may serve You wholeheartedly. Help others to recognize that he/she always serves, never thinking first of him/her self (see Ephesians 6:7).

PASSION FOR GOD:

God, please instill in [baby]'s heart a soul that *"follows hard after You,"* a heart that clings passionately to You (see Psalm 63:8). Give him/her the ability to give him/herself to You in complete abandon; help him/her have passion for You that ignites a fire in other's hearts.

PRAYERFULNESS:

Lord, let [baby]'s life be marked by prayer and prayerfulness, so that he/she may learn to *"pray in the Spirit at all times and on every occasion. Stay alert and be persistent in your prayers…"* (Ephesians 6:18). Make him/her a prayer warrior for his/her family and friends.

GRATITUDE:

Help [baby] to live a life that *"will overflow with thankfulness,"* *"and give thanks for everything to God the Father in the name of our Lord Jesus Christ"* (Colossians 2:7; Ephesians 5:20). Help his/her actions speak volumes to others about all that You have done in and through him/her.

HEART FOR MISSIONS:

Lord, please help [baby] understand that he/she is a missionary every day, wherever he/she goes, whatever he/she does. Give him/her a desire to *"tell of His glory among the nations, His wonderful deeds among all the peoples"* (Psalm 96:3 NASB).

Lord, we know that as Your Word goes forth out of our mouths on [baby]'s behalf, it shall not return to You void. We know that You will accomplish what You plan to do in [baby]'s life and that Your Word will prosper in the things for which You sent it (see Isaiah 55:11).

PROTECTION:

Lord, we know that no weapon formed against [baby] will prosper because You live in him. We know that any tongue that rises up in judgment against [baby] will be condemned by You. This is his/her heritage as Your servant. His/her righteousness is from You (see Isaiah 54:17). You know the plans You have for [baby], You declare plans to prosper him/her and not to harm him/her, plans to give him/her a hope and a future (see Jeremiah 29:11).

Say out loud: *"I give [baby] back to You daily, Lord, recognizing that he/she is a gift You asked me to care for on this earth."*

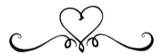

HEART CHECK:

Now that you have completed *Embraced by Grace*, what is now in your heart that wasn't there at the beginning?

Additional Thoughts:

CPSIA information can be obtained at www.ICGtesting.com
Printed in the USA
LVOW09s0831040914

402374LV00001B/3/P